Spelling

Robert Allen is an experienced lexicographer and writer on a wide range of language issues. A former Senior Editor of *The Oxford English Dictionary*, Chief Editor of *The Concise Oxford Dictionary* (1990), Associate Editor of *The Oxford Companion to the English Language* (1992), and Editor of *Pocket Fowler's Modern English Usage* (1999), he has written widely on the use of English in modern times. He now works as a freelance writer and editor, and has written another title for the 'One Step Ahead' series, *One Step Ahead: Punctuation*.

One Step Ahead ...

The *One Step Ahead* series is for all those who want and need to communicate more effectively in a range of real-life situations. Each title provides up-to-date practical guidance, tips, and the language tools to enhance your writing and speaking.

Series Editor: John Seely

Titles in the series

Editing and Revising Texts	Jo Billingham
Essays and Dissertations	Chris Mounsey
Organizing and Participating in Meetings	Judith Leigh
Publicity, Newsletters, and Press Releases	Alison Baverstock
Punctuation	Robert Allen
Spelling	Robert Allen
Words	John Seely
Writing for the Internet	Jane Dorner
Writing Reports	John Seely

Acknowledgements

I should like to thank the series editor, John Seely, for much important advice and encouragement in the writing of this book, which follows an approach to presenting information that was largely devised by him. Thanks are due also to Alysoun Owen and Helen Cox at Oxford University Press for their support and help, and to Beatrice Baumgartner-Cohen for her work on the cartoons.

The text was read by Jenny Ollerenshaw and Lucinda Coventry, and considerably improved as a result. I am most grateful to them, and to Fritz Spiegl for reminding me about Giblet and Sultana (= Gilbert and Sullivan): see page 16. Thanks are also due to Sarah Barrett for her thorough copy-editing of the text.

Robert Allen
Edinburgh
September 2001

Spelling

Robert Allen

Cartoons by Beatrice Baumgartner-Cohen

OXFORD
UNIVERSITY PRESS

OXFORD UNIVERSITY PRESS

Great Clarendon Street, Oxford OX2 6DP

Oxford University Press is a department of the University of Oxford.
It furthers the University's objective of excellence in research, scholarship,
and education by publishing worldwide in
Oxford New York
Auckland Bangkok Buenos Aires Cape Town Chennai
Dar es Salaam Delhi Hong Kong Istanbul Karachi Kolkata
Kuala Lumpur Madrid Melbourne Mexico City Mumbai Nairobi
São Paulo Shanghai Singapore Taipei Tokyo Toronto
with an associated company in Berlin

Oxford is a registered trade mark of Oxford University Press
in the UK and in certain other countries

Published in the United States
by Oxford University Press Inc., New York

British Library Cataloguing in Publication Data
Data available

Library of Congress Cataloging in Publication Data
Data available

ISBN 0-19-860383-5

10 9 8 7 6 5 4 3 2 1

Design and typesetting by David Seabourne
Printed in Spain by Bookprint S.L., Barcelona

Contents

About this book

There are probably three questions in your mind as you start reading this book:

Three key questions

- ■ Why does spelling matter so much?

- ■ How has it got to be so difficult?

- ■ How can I improve?

The answers don't come in quite the same order, but in an order that puts the practicalities of improving your spelling first. The background historical information reflected in the second question is given at the end of the first part of the book.

An action plan

Chapter 1 describes the importance of spelling and gives you an action plan for improving yours.

Rules and patterns

Chapters 2, **3**, and **4** explain how sounds relate to letters, and explore the rules and patterns of English spelling (yes, there are some!).

Looking back

Chapter 5 looks back on how we ended up with such a crazy system.

Finally, there is a reference section at the end which gives you more details about the rules and patterns described in the first part of the book.

A note on British and American spellings

American spelling, like other features of English, differs in some ways from the practice in Britain. In many cases the American rules are more straightforward, and attempt to get rid of some of the inconsistencies and illogicalities that we have in British English.

For example, the word we spell as *licence* (as in *driving licence*) is spelt in American English as *license* (*driver's license*), eliminating the confusing difference between noun (*licence*) and verb (*license*) that exists in British English.

American English uses *-er* endings for words instead of *-re* (e.g. in *center* and *theater*) and shorter spellings such as *ameba* (British *amoeba*) and *catalog* (British *catalogue*). These reduce the number of different ways that you can spell certain sounds, which is exactly what spelling reformers have wanted over the years.

American English also has simpler rules for some inflections (word endings). It does not, for example, make an exception of the letter l by doubling it in words such as *traveler* (as British English does in its spelling *traveller*).

These differences have become more important because of the influence of American English throughout the world, for example on learners of English and on users of the Internet, where American technology predominates.

In spite of the advantages enjoyed by users of American spelling, in Britain people will expect you to use British spellings and will normally regard American usage as unsuitable or incorrect.

In this book the guidance is based on British practice, and important differences in American English are explained when these arise.

Watch out for these signs:

AmE = American English

BrE = British English

For more detailed information on these differences, see the Reference section beginning on page 122.

7

1 | Helping yourself

Why does spelling matter?

You may be surprised to know that spelling has not always mattered as much as it does today. There was a time when people were free to spell words more or less as they wished. But that's not true any more. In fact some people think that nowadays we attach too much importance to spelling. In exams, for example, why should candidates be penalized for spelling mistakes, when they are being tested on something quite different (say history or chemistry)?

The fact is that spelling does matter: the people you want to get a good impression of you are likely to attach a lot of importance to it as a part of the way you present yourself and deliver your message, and you suffer if you are bad at it. People who are poor spellers usually want to do something about it.

Since you are reading this book, spelling must matter to you or at least interest you. This is most likely to be because you want to write well, and because you don't want to give a bad impression to whoever reads what you have written. It matters most in more important and formal contexts like applying for a job or writing a business letter.

Getting the message across

Bad spelling can distract the reader from the main purpose of what you have written, which is to get a message across. The message might simply be giving information, or it might be trying to persuade someone about something. In either case, spelling mistakes stop the reader short, and in extreme cases can even give the wrong meaning or no meaning at all. A piece of writing fails if the reader is constantly put off by bad spelling.

Why is spelling so difficult?

There are many reasons. Here are some important ones:

■ English spelling is full of inconsistencies;

■ some alternative spellings are allowed while others aren't;

■ there are rules and patterns, but lots of exceptions.

Modern English is full of inconsistencies. There is no logical reason why *embarrass* should be spelt with two *r*s and *harass* with only one. It has just worked out that way.

Right and wrong

Most words have a spelling that is correct, so that anything different is wrong. *Accommodation*, for example, should be spelt with two *c*s and two *m*s; but how often have you seen hotel signs that spell it *accomodation*? This is wrong, and *accommodation* is right, and that's all there is to it.

Right and right

But there are some words that can be spelt in two ways, both of them correct. You can spell *judgement* with an *e* or without it (as *judgment*), you can spell *dispatch* with an *i* or an *e* (as *despatch*), and you can spell *encyclopaedia* in a more simple form *encyclopedia*. And there are a whole lot of verbs (action words) ending in *-ize* (such as *privatize*) that can also be spelt *-ise* (*privatise*). All these spellings are correct.

How do you know?

Tip
Keep a notebook for making a note of spellings that you find difficult. See more about this on page 14.

How are you to know when an alternative spelling is correct? One way is to look in a dictionary, which will normally tell you when there is more than one correct way to spell a word. Another is to keep a list of the words of this kind that come up most often. You will find some words of this kind in the list given in the Reference section beginning on page 58, and you can add to these from your own experience.

However, there is no magic formula for telling an acceptable variant spelling from an unacceptable one. The difference depends partly on usage and general acceptability, and not on logic or any set of rules.

Can you learn how to spell?

You can, up to a point, because there are rules and patterns. We will see some of these in Chapter 2. When the rules run out, you have two choices: to rely on memory, and to know where to look for the answer.

Tip
Don't be afraid of having to check difficult spellings. Everyone has to do this from time to time.

Knowing your weaknesses

Very few people are able to spell perfectly. Nearly everyone has some words that they are unsure about and need to check. Ask a random group of people to write down the correct spellings of *acquaintance*, *conscientious*, *harassment*, and *idiosyncrasy* and not many will get them all right.

The important thing is to know when you might be wrong. People often spell words wrongly because they do not realize that there might be another way and they need to check which is right.

Also, recognize which particular types of problem cause you most trouble. They might be systematic problems such as whether to use single or double consonants in words like *accommodate* and *millionaire*, or uncertainty about adding endings to awkward words to form new ones, such as *changeable* and *advisory*.

Using a dictionary

The dictionary is your most useful support in checking and improving your spelling. It will tell you how to spell words and a lot more: what they mean, how you pronounce them, other words that can be made from them (like *traveller* from *travel*), and the other languages that English words come from.

Because a dictionary contains so much information it can sometimes be confusing to use, although publishers have made great efforts in recent years to make the layout clearer and reduce the number of special abbreviations and other conventions that were used in the past to save space.

It's very important to find a dictionary that suits you. Look through several and see how well they help you with particular problems. You may need more than one dictionary, because some dictionaries help you very well with spelling but don't tell you enough about other things you might want to know about, such as the meaning and the origins of words. The answer may be to have a separate dictionary to use for spelling.

There are also special so-called 'spelling dictionaries' that just list words for their spelling and only give you other information when this is needed to help you identify the words you are looking for. One advantage of these is that you can concentrate on the type of information you are looking for, but many people prefer to have the help and reassurance of the rest of the dictionary's information as well.

Some famous English dictionaries

The first three are large historical dictionaries. The other two are one-volume dictionaries of current English that are regularly published in new editions.

Dr Johnson's *Dictionary of the English Language* (1755)

Webster's American Dictionary of the English Language (1828)

The Oxford English Dictionary (1882–1933; second edition 1989)

Chambers' Twentieth Century Dictionary (first published 1901)

The Concise Oxford Dictionary (first published 1911)

Tip

Make sure you have an up-to-date dictionary that suits you.

Opposite you will see the layout of a typical dictionary page. The layout shows a number of features that help you find your way around the information:

■ So-called running heads, the two words printed at the top of each page in large type, tell you which words come first and last on that page. All the words that come alphabetically between those two words will be found on that page.

■ The page is organized into separate entries, each of which has a headword, which is the word being treated in that entry, printed in bold type at the beginning.

■ Usually the headword is followed by a set of characters that tell you how to pronounce the word.

■ Then the part of speech is given, which tells you whether the word is a noun (naming word), verb (action word), adjective (describing word), etc.

■ For some words, different forms, called inflections, are given. Most dictionaries give these systematically when they are irregular or not straightforward. These tell you how to spell the word when it's being used in special ways (e.g. the plural of *hero* is *heroes*, the verb *hurry* becomes *hurries* when you use it after a word like *she* or *the boy*, and the adjective *sticky* becomes *stickier* or *stickiest* when you mean 'more sticky' or 'most sticky').

■ The list of meanings is also important for spelling, to make sure you are looking at the right word. This is particularly true if the problem you are trying to solve is a confusion between two words that sound the same, e.g. between *stationary* and *stationery*. Sometimes the dictionary will also give you example phrases or sentences to show how the word is used.

■ At the end of entries you will sometimes see a list of words that are made from the word you are looking up. These are often very important for their spelling: for example *tranquillity* has two ls (in British English) although the word it is made from, *tranquil*, has only one.

A common problem when you use a dictionary to check a spelling is that you are unsure where to look because you don't know how to spell it! This is especially true if you are doubtful

algorithm | allay 24

labels (annotations): headwords · pronunciation guides · parts of speech · word origins · meanings · inflections · related words · example sentences

algorithm /algariTHam/ ● noun a process or set of rules used in calculations or other problem-solving operations.
– DERIVATIVES **algorithmic** adjective.
– ORIGIN Latin *algorismus*, from an Arabic word meaning 'the man of Ḵwārizm', referring to a 9th-century mathematician.

alias /ayliass/ ● adverb also known as.
● noun 1 a false identity. 2 Computing an identifying label used to access a file, command, or address.
– DERIVATIVES **aliasing** noun.
– ORIGIN Latin, 'at another time, otherwise'.

alibi /alibî/ ● noun (pl. **alibis**) a claim or piece of evidence that one was elsewhere when an alleged act took place.
● verb (**alibis**, **alibied**, **alibiing**) informal provide an alibi for.
– ORIGIN from Latin, 'elsewhere'.

Alice band ● noun a flexible band worn to hold back the hair.
– ORIGIN named after the heroine of *Alice's Adventures in Wonderland* by Lewis Carroll.

alien ● adjective 1 belonging to a foreign country. 2 unfamiliar and distasteful. 3 (of a plant or animal species) introduced from another country and later naturalized. 4 relating to beings from other worlds.
● noun 1 a foreigner. 2 an alien plant or animal species. 3 a being from another world.
– DERIVATIVES **alienness** noun.
– ORIGIN Latin *alienus*, from *alius* 'other'.

alienable ● adjective Law able to be transferred to new ownership.

alienate ● verb 1 cause to feel isolated. 2 lose the support or sympathy of.
– DERIVATIVES **alienation** noun.
– ORIGIN Latin *alienare* 'estrange', from *alius* 'other'.

alight¹ ● verb 1 formal, chiefly Brit. descend from a vehicle. 2 (**alight on**) chance to notice.
– ORIGIN Old English.

alight² ● adverb & adjective 1 on fire. 2 shining brightly.

align ● verb 1 place or arrange in a straight line or into correct relative positions. 2 (**align oneself with**) ally oneself to.
– DERIVATIVES **alignment** noun.
– ORIGIN French *aligner*, from *à ligne* 'into line'.

alike ● adjective similar.
● adverb in a similar way.
– ORIGIN Old English.

alimentary ● adjective providing nourishment or sustenance.
– ORIGIN from Latin *alimentum* 'nourishment'.

alimentary canal ● noun the passage along which food passes through the body.

alimony ● noun chiefly N. Amer. maintenance for a spouse after separation or divorce.
– ORIGIN originally in the sense 'nourishment, means of subsistence': from Latin *alimonia*, from *alere* 'nourish'.

A-line ● adjective (of a garment) slightly flared from a narrow waist or shoulders.

aliphatic /alifattik/ ● adjective Chemistry (of an organic compound) containing an open chain of carbon atoms in its molecule (as in the alkanes), not an aromatic ring.
– ORIGIN from Greek *aleiphar* 'fat'.

aliquot /alikwot/ ● noun 1 a portion of a larger whole, especially a sample taken for chemical analysis or other treatment. 2 (also **aliquot part** or **portion**) Mathematics a quantity which can be divided into another whole number of times.
● verb divide into aliquots; take aliquots from.
– ORIGIN from Latin, 'some, so many'.

alive ● adjective 1 living; not dead. 2 continuing in existence or use. 3 alert and active. 4 having interest and meaning. 5 (**alive with**) swarming or teeming with.
– DERIVATIVES **aliveness** noun.

alkali /alkalî/ ● noun (pl. **alkalis** or **also alkalies**) a compound, such as lime or caustic soda, with particular chemical properties including turning litmus blue and neutralizing or effervescing with acids.
– DERIVATIVES **alkalize** (also **alkalise**) verb.
– ORIGIN originally denoting a saline substance derived from the ashes of plants: from an Arabic word meaning 'fry, roast'.

alkaline ● adjective containing an alkali or having the properties of an alkali; having a pH greater than 7.
– DERIVATIVES **alkalinity** noun.

alkaloid /alkaloyd/ ● noun Chemistry any of a class of nitrogenous organic compounds of plant origin which have pronounced physiological actions on humans.

alkane /alkayn/ ● noun Chemistry any of the series of saturated hydrocarbons including methane, ethane, propane, and higher members.
– ORIGIN from ALKYL.

alkene /alkeen/ ● noun Chemistry any of the series of unsaturated hydrocarbons containing a double bond, including ethylene and propene.
– ORIGIN from ALKYL.

alkyl /alkîl/ ● noun Chemistry a hydrocarbon radical derived from an alkane by removal of a hydrogen atom.
– ORIGIN German *Alkohol* 'alcohol'.

alkyne /alkîn/ ● noun Chemistry any of the series of unsaturated hydrocarbons containing a triple bond, including acetylene.
– ORIGIN from ALKYL.

all ● predeterminer & determiner 1 the whole quantity or extent of: *all her money*. 2 any whatever: *he denied all knowledge*. 3 the greatest possible: *with all speed*.
● pronoun everything or everyone.
● adverb 1 completely. 2 indicating an equal score: *one-all*.
– PHRASES **all along** from the beginning. **all and sundry** everyone. **all but 1** very nearly. 2 all except. **all for** informal strongly in favour of. **all in** informal exhausted. **all in all** on the whole. **all out** using all one's strength or resources. **all over** informal 1 everywhere. 2 informal typical of the person mentioned. **all over the place** informal 1 everywhere. 2 in a state of disorder. **all round 1** in all respects. 2 for or by each person: *drinks all round*. **all told** in total. **at all** in any way. **in all** in total. **on all fours** on hands and knees. **one's all** one's whole strength or resources.
– ORIGIN Old English.

Allah /ala/ ● noun the name of God among Muslims (and Arab Christians).
– ORIGIN Arabic.

allay /alay/ ● verb 1 diminish or end (fear or concern). 2 alleviate (pain or hunger).

---

or wrong about the beginning of the word. For example, *scent* and *psychology* both begin with the same sound, but they are spelt in completely different ways. The same is true of *note*, *knife*, and *pneumonia*.

On page 21 you will find a list of alternative spellings for the same sound at the beginnings of words, so that if you can't find a word where you think it should be, you can try a different letter.

Keep a wordlist

Make a list of the words that cause you most trouble. However many tips you find in this book, there are a lot of words that you simply have to remember by learning them and using them.

You might find it useful to divide your list. Here are three suggestions:

- a master list of all the words that cause you problems;

- a list of words in reading that you thought were wrong but were right or thought were right but were wrong (in both cases record both spellings);

- a list of words organized in patterns, so that words you have problems with are associated with other words that don't cause you a problem. For example, these might be words ending in -*ant* and -*ent*, or -*er* and -*or*.

You will need to review the lists all the time and make changes as your spelling improves. Drop words from the list, or put them into an archive list, once you have mastered them and they are no longer a problem. Other words will need to be added from time to time, especially ones that you don't use very often and may not get on the list at the beginning.

But keep the lists simple, so that they are easy to use. If you keep a record of wrong spellings as well as correct ones, make sure that it is quite clear which are which!

Writing regularly

It is very important to write regularly and use the words that cause you problems, just as you need to speak and use a language when you are learning it.

When you write letters or emails, whether private ones or work ones, take the opportunity to check doubtful spellings and to make use of those words that have caused you problems in the past.

When you are writing, be sure to check the spelling of any words you have doubts about. If they continue to cause you problems, add them to your personal list and keep them there until you are confident about them and can remove them from the list.

Notice spellings when you are reading

A lot depends on what you are reading. Books normally spell accurately and you can therefore be pretty confident about them. Newspapers, which are written in much more of a hurry, make many more mistakes. This gives you an opportunity to test and improve your own knowledge.

Choose an article or feature that interests you. Make a list of the difficult spellings you come across that look right and another list of the ones that look wrong. Then check your lists against a dictionary and see how many in each list you got wrong. Whichever list they are in, you will need to add these to your master list of problem spellings!

You try

Here is a short example for you to try. It is based on an article taken from a national newspaper and contains a few spelling mistakes (specially introduced for this exercise). Make your two lists and then check them against the lists given at the foot of the page.

It is still the most popular museum in London, with six million visitors a year. But 60 per cent of it's visitors are from abroad. Foriegners seem to love the British Museum; to them it is Ancient Greece, Rome and Egypt all rolled into one with a roof over it. The problem is not the visitors themselves, but the wrong kind of visitors.[1]

[1] There are two mistakes: *it's* in the second line should be *its*, and *foriegners* in the third line should be *foreigners*.

Look for mistakes in your own writing

Try to write regularly. Nowadays this doesn't only mean putting pen to paper. We write when we use a computer or send an email.

When you write, look at the patterns in the words you use and keep in mind all the advice given here about knowing when words look right and when they look wrong.

Watch out for words that cause you problems and check them in a dictionary or in your own list. If you get a word wrong, add it to your master list.

Remember that half the battle in improving your spelling is to know when a word might be wrong. Most mistakes occur because people aren't even aware that there is a problem.

Using a spell-checker

If you use a PC or word processor, the program you use for writing (such as Word or Word Perfect) will probably have a spell-checker, which checks spellings for you either automatically as you type or if you ask it to run a check.

Spell-checkers can be useful in finding basic errors, and you should make good use of them when you are writing word-processed documents or emails.

But there are dangers you need to watch out for:

■ Make sure the checker is based on British English and not American (you can normally select this in the options menu).

■ Functionally, most spell-checkers are crude: they have a list of words and if they find a string of letters that aren't in the list they will disallow it. Some checkers are based on poor wordlists and disallow spellings that are in fact correct, either because they are not on its list or because they are on the list in a different spelling which is also correct (as with *judgement* and *judgment*).

Tip
Spell-checkers do not always recognize unusual personal and proper names and can offer comical alternatives, but they are getting better. Gone are the days when we were exhorted to replace Gilbert and Sullivan with 'Giblet and Sultana' and Romeo and Juliet with 'Rodeo and Julies'.

You can usually add to the wordlist and this is something you should do regularly so that it recognizes the words you often use.

■ No spell-checker will spot every mistake, by any means. In particular it won't be much good at finding mistakes arising from confusable words (such as *stationary* and *stationery*) because it allows both spellings and isn't able to distinguish them from the context (although some software developers are working on more context-sensitive checkers).

■ Nor will it spot every typing mistake, if the mistake is also a word it recognizes. For example, a very common mistake is to type *form* instead of *from*, but since *form* is also a word the spell-checker will allow it.

Using the look-spell-cover-write-check method

It is very important to keep writing down words that are difficult. You do this when you are using them, of course, but you should also do it when you are learning them and trying to remember them.

A well-known method of doing this is called LOOK-SPELL-COVER-WRITE-CHECK, which you can use when you are reading:

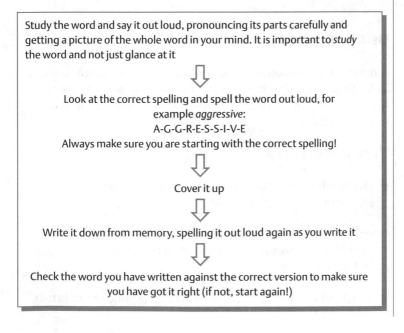

Study the word and say it out loud, pronouncing its parts carefully and getting a picture of the whole word in your mind. It is important to *study* the word and not just glance at it

⇩

Look at the correct spelling and spell the word out loud, for example *aggressive*:
A-G-G-R-E-S-S-I-V-E
Always make sure you are starting with the correct spelling!

⇩

Cover it up

⇩

Write it down from memory, spelling it out loud again as you write it

⇩

Check the word you have written against the correct version to make sure you have got it right (if not, start again!)

Keep doing this from time to time with the problem words on your list.

You can also write down different spellings of the same word so that you get to know which one looks right:

aggressive   agressive   aggresive

Try writing each spelling, the right one and the wrong ones, on small slips of paper. Then put all the slips in a hat or box.

Choose one at random and decide whether it is right or wrong. Either stop when you think you have picked the right spelling, or carry on until you have looked at all the spellings.

Then check whether you are correct.

You will probably find that you can quickly eliminate the spelling that usually looks most wrong, which is *aggresive*. Then you can concentrate on the main area of confusion, which is normally between *aggressive* (right) and *agressive* (wrong). It is usually the double *g* and not the double *s* that people get wrong.

Using mnemonics

A mnemonic (pronounced ne-**mon**-ik; the only common word in English beginning in mn-!) is a rhyme or other set of words that helps you remember how to do something, in this case how to spell a word.

There are some well-known mnemonics:

- **r**hythm **h**as **y**our **t**wo **h**ips **m**oving (for **rhythm**: the initial letters of the mnemonic spell the word);

- one collar and two sleeves (for **necessary**: the initial letters of **collar** and **sleeves** correspond to the number of each letter in the word);

- an island **is land** in water (**island** corresponds to **is land**).

These mnemonics are based on chance word associations:

■ please **add** your **add**ress;

■ a **secret**ary should be able to keep a **secret**;

■ a **govern**ment has to **govern**;

■ **i am** a member of parl**iam**ent;

■ are you at an **age** for marri**age**?

2 Sounds and letters

Tip
Keep a list of
words that have
the same groups
of letters.

You try

Rules and patterns of spelling

English spelling is difficult and troublesome because sounds
can be written in different ways and letters can have more than
one sound. But there are patterns that keep occurring. It will
help you if you can recognize these patterns and be aware of
what lies outside them.

For example, there are groups of letters that crop up in lots of
words. Some of these usually represent the same sound, such
as *ight* in words like *fight*, *light*, *sight*, *tight*, and *alight*. (But the
sound changes when the *i* is combined with another vowel, as
in *straight* and *eight*.)

If you can remember these in groups you will be more likely to
get their spelling right.

Although there are lots of patterns, some words are totally
'one-off' and just have to be learnt: for example *quay* and
colonel. It is a good idea to make a list of the most common of
these as you come across them.

The colonel standing on a quay

How sounds relate to letters

For much of the time turning sounds in our heads into letters on the page is straightforward: in words like *book*, *house*, *send*, and *sniff*, and even in longer words like *garden* and *swimmer*. But there can be complications with some sounds.

A lot of these complications come at the beginning and end of words. And if they come at the beginning, it makes it harder for you to check them in a dictionary because you won't know where to start looking.

It's a good idea to get a grip on which sounds can be represented by more than one letter, so that if one doesn't work when you check it, you know which alternatives to try.

Beginnings

Here are some word beginnings that can cause problems:

Letter	Sound	Spelling 1	Spelling 2	Spelling 3	Spelling 4
c	*as in* can	comic	king	character	
f	*as in* fit	finger	photograph		
g	*as in* get	good	ghost		
j	*as in* jab	jelly	gesture		
n	*as in* name	number	gnome	knife	
r	*as in* rot	range	rhyme	wrap	
s	*as in* sun	seat	city	scene	psychiatrist
t	*as in* tip	tender	thyme	pterodactyl	
w	*as in* war	water	when		
z	*as in* zip	zero	xylophone		

See if you can add to the list. For example, make a list of words beginning with the sound of *n*:

number	gnome	knife
neutral	gnat	knit
never	gnash	knock
note	gnaw	knuckle

Watch out for the spellings that only occur in a few words. For example, you will only find the beginning *gn-* in a handful of words, some of them not used much.

Endings

Some strange spellings occur at the ends of words:

Other endings to watch for

-ct (*indict*)
-bt or -pt (*debt, receipt*)
-lm (*calm, palm*)
-mn (*autumn, solemn*)

See the Reference section on page 112.

m

the sound of m is spelt as *-mb* at the end of some words:
bomb, comb, lamb

and as *-gm* in one word:
phlegm

ough

Some groups of letters seem to defy all the rules and represent different sounds almost from word to word. An example is *ough*, which is pronounced in many different ways in words like *borough*, *bough*, *cough*, *dough*, *thought*, *through*, and *tough*. But even here there is a pattern of sorts, and recognizing this can make the spelling seem less chaotic:

bough	cough	dough	ought	through	tough	borough
plough	trough	though	bought		rough	thorough
		although	sought		enough	
			thought			

Common letter clusters

Some letters often occur together in clusters. These can be vowels (*a, e, i, o, u*) or consonants (the other letters).

Many clusters cause no spelling difficulty because each letter is pronounced separately, e.g. the *b* and *l* in *blind* and the *p* and *r* in *practice*.

But sometimes letters come together to form a single sound, especially when one of these is *h*:

■ *c* makes *ch* (as in *church, character,* and *machine*).

■ *p* makes *ph* (as in *pharmacy* and *sophistry*).

■ *s* makes *sh* (as in *shame* and *hash*).

■ *t* makes *th* (as in *moth* and *this*).

These pairs can also be followed by other letters:

■ *ch* is often followed by *l* (*chloroform*) and *r* (*Christmas*).

■ *ph* is followed by *l* (*phlegmatic*) and *r* (*phrase*).

■ *sh* is followed by *r* (*shrine*).

■ *th* is followed by *r* (*three*).

Vowel clusters

Sometimes when two vowels (*a, e, i, o, u*) come together they are pronounced separately, as in *cooperate* and *theatrical*. More often, though, they form a sound that changes half way through (called a diphthong), as in *pain* and *sound*, or a simple sound (called a pure vowel), as in *sea* and *took*. Getting to know these sounds and spellings can help you to spell thousands of words.

2 Sounds and letters

The sound -ee-

The sound -ee- as in *sleep* is usually spelt in one of three ways:
-ea-, -ee-, and -ie-, and of these ways the first two are the most
common:

ea	*ee*	*ie*
bead	bee	believe
leave	feet	chief
meal	see	field
meat	sleep	siege
peace	teeth	thief
seat	weep	yield

Tip
i comes before *e*
except after *c* but
there *are* exceptions

A well-known rule is that *i* comes before *e* except after *c* in words
that are pronounced -ee- (as in *receive* and *relieve*):

achieve	ceiling
believe	conceit
brief	conceive
fiend	deceive
hygiene	receipt
priest	perceive
siege	receive

But there are exceptions, of which the most important is *seize*.
People often get this wrong because they confuse it with *siege*,
which follows the rule. Beware of these two!

The sound -oh-

The -oh- sound as in *coat* and *cone* is also usually spelt in one of three ways:

oa	*o-e*	*ow*
coat	code	crow
goat	hole	flow
road	pope	grow

There are many other vowel sounds in English. They are usually listed at the beginning of dictionaries to show how the pronunciation system works.

Make a list of these vowel sounds and the various spellings, like the ones above, that can represent them. Then you can link spelling to sound in your mind more effectively.

You try

Here is a list of pairs of vowels (*a, e, i, o, u*) that merge to form a single sound. In some cases the combined sound varies from one word to another. See which sounds can also be spelt in other ways, like the ones above:

ae	as in	*aeroplane*	*archaeology*	
ai	as in	*main*	*pair*	
ea	as in	*cheap*	*bear*	
ee	as in	*meet*		
ei	as in	*receive*	*rein*	
eu	as in	*feud*		
ie	as in	*friend*	*lie*	*siege*
oa	as in	*boat, roar*	*roar*	
oe	as in	*oestrogen, amoeba*		
oi	as in	*coil*		
ou	as in	*bound*	*ought*	
ui	as in	*fruit*		

other -*ough* sounds: see table on page 22.

Long and short vowels

You can see in some of the examples above that a silent -*e* at the end of a word can have the effect of 'lengthening' the vowel in words like *code* and *pope* (compare *cod* and *pop*, which have short vowels). This works with other vowels too: compare *mat* and *mate*, *din* and *dine*, *tun* and *tune*.

There is another useful pattern to note: double consonants usually keep a preceding vowel short, as in *cliff*, *cross*, and *jazz*. (There are a few exceptions, such as *call* and *ball*, which have a long vowel sound.)

You try

See if you can find other words that fit into these patterns.

Problem areas and how to deal with them

Double and single letters

A lot of the difficulty people have with spelling is to do with whether you write one letter or two in words like *disappoint* and *accommodation*. which are often misspelt *dissapoint* and *accomodation*.

Embarrass (with two *rs*) and *harass* (with one *r*) always cause problems, and so do *occurrence* and *tranquillity* (which confusingly is spelt *tranquility* with one *l* in American English).

In many cases you just have to learn the correct spellings, but there are a few tips that are worth noting. For example, if you remember that *disappear* and *disappoint* are made from the prefix *dis-* (not *diss-*) and the familiar words *appear* and *appoint*, you should be less likely to get them wrong.

You will find more advice about analysing words in this way in the next part of this chapter, and a list of words of this type in the Reference section.

Tip
Embarrass has two *rs* but *harass* only has one.

AmE
For other differences see page 122.

Prefixes are explained on page 43.

See page 97.

Coping with confusables

Confusables are words that are similar in sound but spelt differently, for example *bare* (= naked) and *bear* (the animal, and the verb as in *I can't bear it*) and the trio *vain* (= proud), *vane* (as in *weathervane*), and *vein* (carrying blood in the body).

Some confusables are very basic 'function' words that we use all the time, such as *it's* (= it is or it has) and *its* (the possessive pronoun), and *who's* (= who is or who has) and *whose* (as in *whose book is this?*).

Tip
Words like *bare* and *bear* that are pronounced the same are also called homophones (from Greek *homos* 'the same' and *phone* 'sound').

Confusing homophones is one of the most common types of misspelling.

For more examples see page 62.

Of course its beauty is greater than its speed

But it's speed I find beautiful!

For Sale

The best way to master these is to associate them with their meaning and use, i.e. to learn them in context. Here are some very common examples of this type of confusion.

Everyday confusables

Who's and whose

You use *who's* in sentences like these:

Who's been using my desk?
I don't know **who's** to blame.

Think about what these sentences mean, and how the word *who's* is used in each. In the first sentence, *who's* stands for *who has*, and the sentence could be expanded as follows:

Who has been using my desk?

In the second sentence, *who's* stands for *who is*, and the sentence could be expanded as follows:

I don't know **who is** to blame.

The apostrophe is used to represent missing letters, either the *i* of *is* or the *ha* of *has*. Once you are aware of this you can remember the correct spelling better because you know the reason for it.

Tip
Apostrophes in words like *who's* and *didn't* stand for missing letters.

Knowing this helps you put the apostrophe in the right place.

Whose is used in similar types of sentences (hence the confusion!) but with an entirely different meaning. You use *whose* in sentences like these:

Whose desk is this?
I don't know whose it is.

In these sentences you cannot expand *whose* to *who is* or *who has* because this would produce gibberish. Also, you can use *whose* by itself (as in the second sentence above), but you can't do this with *who's*.

Its and it's

This pair of homophones probably causes more trouble than any other spelling problem in English. This is because the spelling is a bit more complicated than it was for *who's* and *whose*.

You use *it's* in sentences like these:

It's been raining.
I don't know if it's here.

Again, the apostrophe is used to show that a letter or group of letters is missing. So *it's* can be expanded to *it has* in the first sentence and to *it is* in the second.

You use *its* in sentences like these:

The cat was licking its paws.

Here, *its* is a possessive word, showing what something belongs to. Because it is possessive, it is easy to be misled into thinking that *its* should have an apostrophe here too, but it is a word in its own right like *my*, *your*, *his*, *her*, *our*, and *their*. If you remember the possessive word *its* as part of this group, it will be more obvious that an apostrophe would be an intruder, because none of the others has one.

Their, there, and they're

The best way to show the differences between these homophones is to use them in the same sentence:

*Their house is over **there**, and **they're** sitting in the garden.*

The first one, *their*, is a possessive word. The second, *there*, indicates the position of something, and the third, *they're*, is short for *they are* in the same way as *who's* and *it's* are shortenings.

If you can remember these associations you will be able to spell each of the three homophones correctly. If not, you will see that the three words *their*, *there*, and *they're* appear in alphabetical order in the sentence, so if you can remember the sentence it shouldn't take long to identify each correct spelling.

To, too, and two

Again, the best way to distinguish these is by using them all in the same sentence in alphabetical order:

*I'd like **to** go **to** the shops **too**, but it's **too** late to get there by **two**.*

(*To* and *too* appear twice each in the sentence to show the two ways they are used!)

Other confusables

Sometimes pairs of words that are spelt with small but important differences can cause confusion. In many cases they are related in form and origin (for example, *stationary* and *stationery*).

Finding out about the origins of words will often help you. For example, *cereal* (the food) comes from the name *Ceres*, the Roman goddess of agriculture, whereas a *serial* is a *series* of things. Most household dictionaries give information on the origins of words .

Tip
Remember confusable words in context, either in a list of similar words or in a pair of sentences.

Tip
Find out the origin of each word and how it was formed.

Here are some common examples:

complement (= extra thing)	*compliment* (= praise)
hoard (= large supply)	*horde* (= crowd of people)
principal (= chief)	*principle* (a truth or rule)
stationary (= not moving)	*stationery* (paper etc.)
storey (of building)	*story* (tale)

For a longer list of confusable words see page 62.

-c- for noun and -s- for verb

Some words of Latin origin that have noun and verb forms differ between the two: -c- in the noun and -s- in the verb, for example *practice* (noun, as in *a hard practice*) and *practise* (verb, as in *to practise hard*). This is easy to remember because the letters are in alphabetical order: C-N(OUN)-S-V(ERB). Some words differ in pronunciation too, for example *advice* and *advise*.

Examples:

Noun	Verb
advice : *I'll give you some advice*	advise : *who will advise me?*
licence : *a television licence*	license : *licensed to serve drinks*
practice : *piano practice*	practise : *I must practise my French*
prophecy : *a false prophecy*	prophesy : *He has prophesied disaster*

Note that the rules are different in American English. For example, *license* is a noun (as in *a driver's license*) as well as a verb (as in *to be licensed*). There is more information about these differences in the Reference section.

AmE see the Reference section on page 122.

Words of foreign origin

Strictly speaking, over half of the English vocabulary is of 'foreign' origin in the sense that it does not come from Anglo-Saxon, an early ancestor of modern English. Words such as *egg*, *skull*, and *window* come from Old Norse, the language of the Vikings. And thousands of Latin-based words were introduced into English from French after the Norman conquest of 1066, such as *council*, *liberty*, *conflict*, and *important*.

There is another type of more truly 'foreign' words, which have come into English in more recent times and have still kept a spelling that is close to the language they came from. These often cause problems because they are not typically English in form and therefore don't fit very well with the rules of English spelling.

For example, the word *ski* is a Norwegian word. When it is used as a verb (action word) in English its forms are (he or she) *skis*, *skied*, and *skiing*. This is simply a matter of custom, because the few other verbs ending in *-i* in English usually have a third-person singular form in *-es*, for example (an aircraft) *taxies*. The reason *ski* behaves differently may be to avoid confusion with the plural of *sky*; at any rate, this is a good way of remembering the correct spelling of *ski*.

For more words, see page 113.

There are a lot of mainly technical words that come from Greek and Latin and still have their original ending:

■ words ending in -*a*, -*um*, or -*us*, for example *addendum, arena, consortium, formula, hiatus, maximum, status;*

■ words ending in -*x*, -*is*, and -*ma*, for example *apex, appendix, helix, index, oasis, stigma.*

Many of these words form English plurals by simply adding -*s*, especially when they are more familiar words or are in general use: *arenas, consortiums, formulas, appendixes, indexes, maximums, referendums, stigmas.*

When words of this kind are used in more technical contexts, however, they tend to keep their original Latin plurals:

singular	plural	example
-*a*	-*ae*	*formulae*
-*ex*	-*ices*	*apices*
-*is*	-*es*	*oases*
-*ix*	-*ices*	*indices*
-*ma*	-*mata*	*stigmata*
-*um*	-*a*	*addenda*
-*us*	-*i*	*hiatuses*

An exception is *genus*, which has a plural form *genera*.

You will notice that some words have two plural forms: one for general use and the other for technical use. An example is *index*, which has the plural *indexes* for the meaning to do with books and *indices* for the meanings to do with finance and statistics. *Appendix* has a plural *appendices* when referring to parts of a book.

For more words of foreign origin *see* page 113.

Word-based strategies

Recognizing syllables and breaking long words into elements

Tip
Breaking words down into syllables is rather like a game of charades: you mime each syllable as if it were a separate word. The difference is that charades is based entirely on sounds.

You try

Use this method to isolate the syllables, then check the spelling of each syllable.

One of the problems with long words is that it is difficult to think of the whole word at once and get an overall mental picture of it. A way of overcoming this problem is to break down long words into syllables. A syllable is the shortest part of the word that can be pronounced separately; it contains one of the vowels *a*, *e*, *i*, *o*, *u*, and *y*, and usually one or more of the consonants *b*, *c*, *d*, *f*, etc. as well. Sometimes it contains more than one vowel pronounced together (e.g. *a* and *i* in *rain*), but a syllable never contains consonants without a vowel.

Words like *book*, *chair*, and *house* are one-syllable words. *Dagger*, *garden*, and *shopping* each have two syllables:

dag-ger
gar-den
shop-ping

Longer words can be broken up into several syllables:

remember   re-mem-ber
circumstance   cir-cum-stance
melancholy   me-lan-cho-ly
privatization   pri-va-ti-za-tion

Each syllable will need its own musical note

It's rather like trying to remember a long telephone number. If you think of it as one string of numbers it's very difficult to keep them all in your head. But if you think of it as an area code (such as 020 for London or 0131 for Edinburgh) followed by a group code (e.g. 667) and then the individual number (e.g. 2395) it becomes a lot easier to remember. The parts of a telephone number are like the syllables of a long word.

One way of seeing how many syllables there are in a word is to sing it: each syllable will need its own musical note.

The point of breaking a word into syllables is that you can then think about how to spell each part by itself, and the task becomes much more manageable. If you constantly misspell a word, you can identify the particular syllable you always get wrong and concentrate on that.

For example, if you tend to misspell words like *disappear* and *disappoint*, you can isolate the syllables *dis-ap-pear* and *dis-ap-point* and see which part causes the problem. In this case, it will probably be the end of the first syllable *dis-* and the end of the second syllable *ap-*. Knowing how the word breaks down will help you to locate the difficulty and put it right. Trying to cope with a word like *disappoint* all in one go is much more daunting and much harder to remember.

How the origin and meaning of words can help you to spell them

Obviously no one can be expected to know the source of every English word, but knowing something about the words that you find hard to spell can be a great help.

For example, you might find it difficult to distinguish between *separate* and *desperate*, the first of which has one *e* and two *a*s and the second two *e*s and one *a*. Both words come from Latin roots:

- *Separate* comes from Latin words *se* meaning 'apart' and *parare* meaning 'to prepare': the meaning elements are therefore 'to prepare something apart', i.e. to divide it or separate it. So you don't even have to know the Latin word; if you know that *separate* is related to *prepare* you can remember the syllable *-par-* that is common to both words.

■ *Desperate* comes from Latin words *de* meaning 'away' or 'not' and *sperare* meaning to 'hope', i.e. it means 'deprived of hoping'.

It also helps to know the relations between English words. For example, if you have trouble with the ending of words of the type *circular*, *popular*, and *vulgar*, it helps to relate them to their corresponding noun forms *circularity*, *popularity*, and *vulgarity*, where the choice of the vowel *a* is much more obvious.

Knowing when words look right

Being able to tell when a word looks right or, just as importantly, doesn't look right can be very helpful. Many people make spelling mistakes because they are not aware of a problem and haven't noticed that a word they have used doesn't look right.

There are several ways of developing techniques for recognizing words that are wrong:

Tip
Keeping a personal wordlist in a notebook will help with these activities: *see* page 14.

■ Make a point of concentrating on how the difficult words look when you come across them in your reading.

■ Try writing out a word you misspell in its wrong form and compare it visually with the correct spelling.

■ Learn to recognize combinations of letters that don't often occur in English and are probably wrong in the word you have used.

■ Make lists of words in groups according to their spelling patterns, for example all the words with a double consonant such as *-ll-* in them or all the words that end in *-ension* and *-ention*. Then you will begin to recognize them as belonging to a family of words rather than as isolated cases.

Endings and changes

4

In this chapter we will look at the problems caused by different kinds of endings that some words have, and in particular:

- when there is a choice of spelling, e.g. between -*ance* and -*ence*;

- when endings (and occasionally beginnings) that you add to words affect their spelling, e.g. *deny, denies, deniable.*

Endings have a special role in turning words of one kind into words of another kind. For example, -*ance* and -*ence* turn verbs (doing words) and adjectives (describing words) into nouns (naming words): *endurance* means 'the act or process of enduring', and *obedience* means 'being obedient'.

Some words that have these endings do not have such an obvious connection with a verb or other word because they have come into English ready-formed from another language (often via French from Latin): for example, *distance*.

The problem of choice

Sometimes the same ending is spelt in different ways, for example *credible* and *laughable*, *accuracy* and *ecstasy*, and *actor, burglar,* and *builder.*

In this section, we will look at some endings that have more than one spelling and suggest ways of coping with them. The chief problem here is that there are often no useful rules to guide you, or there are so many rules and so many exceptions that they simply confuse you. But there are a few patterns with some of them.

You will find fuller lists of the words described in this chapter on page 78.

Endings with a choice of spelling

-*able* and -*ible*
-*acy* and -asy
-*ance* and -*ence*
-*ant* and -*ent*
-*ary*, -*ery*, and -*ory*
-*er*, -*or*, and -*ar*
-*tion*, -*sion*, and -*cion*

You will find more endings, including -*ise* and -*ize*, on page 78.

Watch out for the tip boxes!

4 Endings and changes

Tip
You are more likely to
be right if you chose
-able, but check in
your dictionary!
-able is used to make
new words, e.g.
programmable.

For spelling problems
with -able, see
page 44.

Tip
If you can't split the
word into parts that
make sense, the
ending is likely to
be -ible:

adaptable =
adapt+able
poss–ible ≠
poss + ible

Tip
There are very few
nouns ending in -asy.
These three are the
only common ones.

Tip
It helps to recognize
word families.
Nouns and adjectives
that come from verbs
ending in -y or -ate
normally end in
-ance: defy, defiance,
defiant; tolerate,
tolerant, tolerance.

-able and *-ible*

These endings occur in adjectives that mean 'able to be—' or
something like it: for example, *adaptable* means 'able to be
adapted' and *digestible* means 'able to be digested'.

adaptable   credible
desirable   digestible
laughable   invisible

You will find many more words in the Reference section beginning on page 78.

When a word ends in *-able*, the core part of the word is usually
a distinct word in itself:

adorable   forgettable   measurable
bearable   manageable   payable

There are far fewer words ending in *-ible* than in *-able*, and the
part that comes before *-ible* is not usually a word in its own right:

credible   invisible   tangible
fallible   possible   terrible

-acy and *-asy*

accuracy   ecstasy
literacy   fantasy
supremacy   idiosyncrasy

-ance and *-ence*

appearance   confidence
elegance   existence
significance   innocence

-ant and *-ent*

arrogant   confident
defiant   eminent
extravagant   lenient

38

Some words of this type cause difficulty because they are both nouns (naming words) and adjectives (describing words) and their spellings vary between the two. Fortunately, there are not many of these, and the only one you are likely to need regularly is:

dependant (noun, as in *have you any dependants?*)
dependent (adjective, as in *success is dependent on hard work*).

-ary, -ery, and -ory

Words ending in *-ary* and *-ory* can be adjectives (describing words) or nouns (naming words), but *slippery* is the only common adjective ending in *-ery* apart from those that are based on words ending in *-er* (e.g. *shivery, thundery*)

arbitrary	bravery
commentary	lottery
military	surgery

-er, -or, and -ar

builder	actor	beggar
foreigner	investor	burglar
jeweller	spectator	liar
opener	visitor	pedlar

-tion, -sion, and -cion

attraction	expansion	coercion
section	diversion	suspicion

When choosing between *-tion*, *-sion*, and *-cion*, notice that *-sion* often follows an *n* or *r*:

apprehension	conversion
extension	diversion

If the ending is pronounced like the *s* in *measure*, the spelling is *-sion*:

adhesion	incision
confusion	persuasion

Tip
Dependant or *dependent*?

A good way of remembering this spelling is to think of **a** *dependant*: the *a*'s match.

Tip
Most words ending in *-ery* are nouns.

Tip
There are very few 'doer' nouns ending in *-ar*. These four are the most common.

Tip
Coercion and *suspicion* are the only common words ending in *-cion*, but there are many that end in *-ician*, e.g. *magician, musician, politician*. These all relate to words ending in *-ic* or *-ics* or *-ical*: *magic, music, politics*.

If the ending is pronounced -*shun* and comes after a vowel (*a, e, i, o, u*) the spelling will nearly always be -*tion*:

accretion	pollution
nation	position
inhibition	ration

Exceptions are words ending in -*ssion*, which are based on words ending in -ss, e.g. *discussion, percussion, possession*

Words that are based on words ending in -*ate* are spelt -*ation*:

create	creation
donate	donation
educate	education
meditate	meditation
related	relation
rotate	rotation

Words that are based on words ending in -*vert* end in -*sion*:

convert	conversion
divert	diversion
introvert	introversion
invert	inversion
pervert	perversion
revert	reversion

Tip
It helps to know where these endings came from. If you don't know much Latin or Old English (and many people don't!), a good dictionary that gives word origins will help you.

There are two endings -*able* and -*ible* because they come from Latin words ending in -*abilis* and -*ibilis*. In the same way, the spellings -*er*, -*or*, and -*ar* come from different Latin endings, and the noun endings -*ance* and -*ence* come from Latin forms -*antia* and -*entia*.
It also helps to think of word families: for example the connections between *create* and *creation*, *divert* and *diversion*, and *magic* and *magician* all provide clues to the spellings.

Words that change because of grammar

Why some words change

A common form of spelling problem occurs when words change their form to fit the sentence you use them in.

For example, the word *stop* is simple enough, but sometimes you have to change its form to *stopped* or *stopping*: *She stopped the car | Why are you stopping the car?*

The endings for *stop* follow a rule or pattern, because you have to double the *p* at the end. But you don't always double the final letter—for example *stoop*, which has a long vowel *oo*, has the forms *stooped* and *stooping* with a single *p*.

> These special endings you give to words are called 'inflections'.

1 running   2 stopping   3 stooping

And if you want to talk about more than one *box* or *house* you have to use plural forms: *boxes, houses*.

These are the main things you have to do to words to make them fit the grammar of sentences:

Adding -s or -es

You do this to make plurals of nouns (*cats, boxes*) and endings of verbs that refer to a person or thing you are speaking about (the so-called 'third person'), e.g. *stops* as in *when the bus stops* and *catches* as in *I hope John catches the ball.*

Normally you add *s*, but when the word ends in *-s, -x, -z, -sh,* or *-ch* (pronounced as in *church*), you add *-es* (*hisses, fixes, fizzes, pushes, crunches*).

> ### 's and s'
>
> Another form of ending that causes problems is the possessive form, as in *a day's journey.*
>
> The basic rule is to add 's to the noun:
>
> *a girl's room*
> *the children's shoes*
>
> When the noun is plural and ends in s, you just add an apostrophe:
>
> *their parents' room*
> *in three days' time*

Adding -ed and -ing to verbs

You add -ed to verbs (action words) to make them refer to the past (she looked beautiful / have you looked?), and you add -ing to make the form that refers to continuous action in the present, as why are you laughing?

Adding -er and -est to adjectives and adverbs

Another adjective ending is -ish: **smallish**

Describing words (adjectives and adverbs) such as small and soon also have endings to give them special meanings. These endings are -er and -est: smaller means 'more small' and smallest means 'most small'; sooner means 'more soon' and soonest means 'most soon'.

How these endings affect spelling

All the endings we have been looking at in this chapter can cause particular problems:

The consonants affected are b, d, f, g, l, m, n, p, r, s, t, z.

■ When the word ends in a single consonant, you double it in words with a short single-letter vowel like stopped, stopping and bigger, biggest, biggish, but not in words with a long sound made from two vowels like stooped, stooping, and broader, broadest.

You will find fuller rules and lists to help you with these words on page 98.

■ You double the consonant in words like allotted and allotting (with the 'stress' or emphasis on the -ot-) but not in words like balloted and balloting (with the stress on the earlier syllable ball-).

■ When the word ends in an e, you normally drop the e before the ending as in the verbs baking and changing. and the adjectives larger, largest, and largish.

For endings of words ending in -o, see page 98.

■ When the word ends in another vowel (especially i or o), you sometimes add an e before the ending, as in buffaloes but not banjos, and in videoes (as a verb: he always videoes the programme) but not videos (as a noun: a pile of videos).

■ You sometimes change the stem of the word (i.e. the part without the ending), especially a final *y* (after a consonant), to *i*, as in the adjective *early, earlier, earliest*, the verb *envy, envies, envied*, and the noun *pony, ponies*.

For words ending in -*y, see* page 101.

Adding prefixes and suffixes

There are other groups of letters, called prefixes and suffixes, that you can add to words to change their meaning. Prefixes come at the beginning, and suffixes come at the end. For example, the prefix *re-* means 'again', as in *rebuild* and *reincarnation*, and the suffix *-ly* makes adverbs (words meaning 'in a—way'), as in *loudly* and *happily*.

Some common suffixes

-able, -ible = able to be (*eatable, edible*)

-al used to make adjectives (*magical*)

-ance, -ence used to make nouns (*appearance, existence*)

-en used to make verbs (*blacken, happen*)

-er, -or, -ar = someone who does (*builder, actor, pedlar*)

-er, -est = more, most (*bigger, biggest*)

-ess = female (*lioness*)

-ful = full, full of (*cupful, beautiful*)

-ish = rather (*largish*)

-hood, -ity, -ment, -ness used to make nouns (*brotherhood, scarcity, merriment, firmness*)

-ish = somewhat (*largish*)

-ize, -ise used to make verbs (*privatize*)

-less = lacking (*careless*)

-ly used to make adverbs (*largely*)

-ous used to make adjectives (*industrious*)

-tion used to make nouns (*abbreviation*)

-y used to make adjectives (*noisy, muddy*)

Some common prefixes

ante- = before (*anteroom*)

anti- = against (*antifreeze*)

co- = with (*cooperate*)

de- = away (*de-ice*)

dis- = not (*disinclined*)

ex- = former (*ex-president*)

in- = not (*insane*): also written as *il-* (*illegal*), *im-* (*impossible*), *ir-* (*irregular*)

mis- = wrong (*misbehave*)

non- = not (*non-smoking*)

pre- = before (*prehistoric*)

pro- = forward (*proceed*)

pro- = in favour of (*pro-life*)

re- = again (*recharge*)

trans- = across (*transatlantic*)

un- = not (*unhappy*)

Adding prefixes

Tip
Use a hyphen to avoid awkward collisions of letters after prefixes, e.g.

de-ice
re-enact
non-Christian
micro-organism

You will find more on hyphens on page 115.

Prefixes cause little trouble because they are usually just added to the beginnings of words, but with some prefixes you need a hyphen if the following word begins with a capital letter (e.g. *un-American*).

ex- and *non-* are usually used with a hyphen: *ex-wife*, *non-existent*.

anti- and *co-* are usually written without a hyphen: *antifreeze*, *cooperate*. But use a hyphen if the word is very long: *anti-marketeer*. If in doubt, look in your dictionary.

You often need a hyphen when a prefix ends in a vowel (e.g. *re-*, *micro-*) and is joined to a word beginning with the same vowel or one that might confuse the sound. If in doubt, check the spelling in your dictionary.

> **Tip**
> Recognizing the prefix will help you with words like *disapprove* (= *dis* + *approve*) and *immortal* (= *im-* + *mortal*)

Adding *-ly*, *-ness*, *-ment*, and *-hood*

Tip
You add *-ly* to adjectives (describing words) to make adverbs (words that tell you how something is done): *large*, *largely*; *quick*, *quickly*.

The main area of difficulty affecting all these suffixes is with words ending in *-y*. When the *y* comes after a consonant (any letter other than the vowels *a, e, i, o, u*) the *y* changes to *i* : *happy*, *happily*, *happiness*, *merry*, *merrily*, *merriment*, *hardy*, *hardily*, *hardihood*.

> **Tip**
> You add *-ness*, *-ment*, and *-hood* to adjectives to make nouns: *dark*, *darkness*; *content*, *contentment*; *brother*, *brotherhood*. Another noun ending is *-ity*: *paucity*, *insanity* (which drops the *e* of *insane* because *-ity* begins with a vowel).

Adding *-able* and *-er*

These words behave in the same way as for the endings *-ed* and *-ing* explained on page 42.

Both these suffixes that can be added freely to make new words, e.g. *programmable*, *programmer*.

When the word ends in a single consonant (chiefly *b, d, f, g, l, m, n, p, r, s, t, z*), you double the consonant when it follows a single-letter vowel with the stress on it (e.g. *swimmer* and *forgettable*), but not when the stress is on an earlier vowel (e.g. *opener*) or when the sound is a long one made of two vowels (e.g. *repeatable*).

When the word ends in a *y* after a consonant you change this to *i*: *copy*, *copier*, *copiable*.

When the word ends in *e*, you often drop the *e* before *-able* (e.g. *lovable*), but you keep the *e* if this is needed to preserve the sound of the first part of the word, e.g. *blameable*, *changeable* (otherwise the *g* would have a hard sound as in *gable*)

> You also drop the *e* before other suffixes beginning with a vowel, e.g. *largish*, *latish*

Adding *-ful*

Words meaning 'full of—' end in *-ful* and not *-full*, e.g. *beautiful*, *cupful*. Some of these words are adjectives (describing words: *a beautiful day*) and others are nouns (naming words: *a cupful of water*).

Many of these words are so familiar in their own right that we do not always think of them in terms of words with a suffix, but the spelling problems are of the same kind.

The following lists show adjectives and nouns separately:

Adjectives

> For more examples *see* page 110.

beautiful	graceful	hurtful	pitiful	spiteful
cheerful	harmful	merciful	playful	tactful
dreadful	helpful	painful	plentiful	thankful
fanciful	hopeful	peaceful	scornful	useful

Most of these words are made up of the ending *-ful* added to a noun, e.g. *help + ful = helpful*. Nouns ending in *-y* following a consonant (any letter other than the vowels *a, e, i, o, u*) change the *-y* to *i*, e.g. *fanciful*, *pitiful*, *plentiful*.

> **Tip**
> Note *skilful* (two *l*s) in BrE, *skillful* (three *l*s) in AmE

Nouns

bellyful	cupful	houseful	pocketful
bottleful	glassful	mouthful	roomful
carful	handful	plateful	spoonful

> **Tip**
> Nouns ending in *-ful* have plural forms ending in *-fuls*:
>
> *cupfuls*
> *handfuls*
> *spoonfuls*

Doubling of consonants before endings

Here is a summary of the rules about doubling a final consonant when you add an ending to a word, as in words like
begging (from *beg*), *occurrence* (from *occur*), and *sitter* (from *sit*).

The consonants
mainly affected here
are *b*, *d*, *f*, *g*, *l*, *m*, *n*,
p, *r*, *s*, *t*, and *z*.

This problem only arises with single consonants at the end of
the core word (*beg*, *occur*, and *sit*) when the word-ending begins
with a vowel (*a*, *e*, *i*, *o*, *u*), e.g. *-able*, *-ance*, *-ed*, *-er*, *-ing*, etc.

You double the consonant:

- in words of one syllable, when the consonant follows a
  single-letter vowel:
  stop, stopped, stopping, stoppable, stopper;

Words ending in a
single *l* following a
single-letter vowel
always double the *l*
in BrE, regardless of
the stress: *level*,
*levelled, levelling,
leveller*

But in AmE the *l* is
not doubled: *level*,
leveled, etc.

- in words of two or more syllables, when the consonant
  follows a single-letter vowel which has the main stress or
  emphasis on it (as in *regret* and *occur* but not *target* and *offer*,
  which have the main stress on the first syllables *tar-* and *-off*):
  regret, regretted, regretting, regrettable
  (but *target, targeted, targeting*)
  occur, occurred, occurring, occurrence
  (but *offer, offered, offering, offerable*).

For words ending in
-*c* (e.g. *panic*), see
page 104.

Preference has only
one *r* because the
stress is on the first
syllable *pref-*, unlike
*prefer, preferred,
preferring*.

Looking back: how spelling got to be so difficult

More sounds than letters

All language exists as speech long before any written form appears. We would like the spelling of words to match the way we pronounce them, whereas in English for much of the time it doesn't seem to correspond at all. This is partly because we use an alphabet, called the Roman alphabet, that was originally devised for Latin, an older language with patterns of sounds and grammatical structures that differ from English.

The Roman alphabet was fine for Romans

There are over forty sounds in English but only twenty-six letters to represent them. Some letters simply represent one sound, for example *f, l, m,* and *z*. But most letters can represent more than one sound. For example, the consonant *c* is pronounced differently in the three words *cake, city,* and (combined with *h*) *church.* The vowel *e* is different in the words *den, pretty,* and *patient,* and sometimes it is not pronounced at all, especially at the end of words (as in *come* and *dance*).

Letters have to double up

In order to cope with the large number of sounds, two or more letters are often used together to form one sound: vowels as in *meet* and *soak* and consonants as in *ch, sh,* and *th.* The same set of letters can represent different sounds (although there are variations in some regional accents): *oo* stands for three different sounds in the words *book, soon,* and *cooperate,* and *ch* stands for two different sounds in *character* and *church.*

It works the other way round, too. The same sound can be written by different letters; for example, the words *sleeve, weave, receive,* and *relieve* all rhyme, but the syllables that sound the same are spelt in different ways; furthermore, two of the spellings are the same two letters put in a different order, which is bound to cause confusion. The -ee- sound in these word can be written in other ways too, as in the words *people, quay,* and *machine.*

Some letters are silent

Other letters can, in some positions, have no pronunciation at all, for example *g* in words like *gnome, k* in words like *knife,* the *t* in *castle* and the *n* in *autumn* and *column,* and *r* in hundreds of words ending in *-er* and *-or* such as *butter* and *anchor* (except in some varieties of English and in all varieties when they are followed by a word beginning with a vowel).

A gnome holds a knife in autumn

Pronunciation has changed

Some spelling difficulties have arisen because the pronunciation of words has changed over the centuries since they were first written down, so that the mismatch between pronunciation and spelling has widened.

The most far-reaching of these changes is known as the Great Vowel Shift, which took place in the fourteenth century in the lifetime of the poet Chaucer. During this process, which was remarkably rapid, the number of 'long' vowels (for example the one in *heed* as distinct from the one in *head*) was reduced from seven to the five we use today (in the words *bean, barn, born, boon,* and *burn*). Before this change, the word *life* was pronounced as we now pronounce *leaf*, and *name* was pronounced as two syllables to rhyme with *farmer*. After the change, the spellings stayed the same, which explains why we spell so many words with an *e* at the end that we do not pronounce any more.

Words from Anglo-Saxon

The reason for all these complications lies partly in the way English has developed over many centuries, drawing on many other languages to build up its stock of words. A lot of the words we use today are genuinely English in the sense that they come from Anglo-Saxon, the language spoken in Britain from the fifth to the eleventh centuries: examples include *go, good,* and *house.* But many others come from other languages.

174   THE CANTERBURY TALES

Arrayed after the lusty seson soote
Lightly, for to pleye and walke on foote,   390
Nat but with fyve or sixe of hir meynee;
And in a trench forth in the park gooth she.
   The vapour which that fro the erthe glood
Made the sonne to seme rody and brood;
But nathelees it was so fair a sighte   395
That it made alle hire hertes for to lighte,
What for the seson and the morwenynge,
And for the foweles that she herde synge.
For right anon she wiste what they mente
Right by hir song, and knew al hire entente.
   The knotte why that every tale is toold,   401
If it be taried til that lust be coold
Of hem that han it after herkned yoore,
The savour passeth ever lenger the moore,
For fulsomnesse of his prolixitee;   405
And by the same resoun, thynketh me,
I sholde to the knotte condescende,
And maken of hir walkyng soone an ende.
   Amydde a tree, for drye as whit as chalk,
As Canacee was pleyyng in hir walk,   410
Ther sat a faucon over hire heed ful hye,
That with a pitous voys so gan to crye
That all the wode resouned of hire cry.
Ybeten hadde she hirself so pitously
With bothe hir wynges til the rede blood   415
Ran endelong the tree ther-as she stood.
And evere in oon she cryde alwey and shrighte,
And with hir beek hirselven so she prighte
That ther nys tygre, ne noon so crueel beest
That dwelleth outher in wode or in forest,   420
That nolde han wept, if that he wepe koude,
For sorwe of hire, she shrighte alwey so loude.
For ther nas nevere yet no man on lyve,
If that I koude a faucon wel discryve,
That herde of swich another of fairnesse,   425
As wel of plumage as of gentillesse
Of shap, of al that myghte yrekened be.
A faucon peregryn thanne semed she
Of fremde land; and everemoore, as she stood,
She swowneth now and now for lak of blood,
Til wel neigh is she fallen fro the tree.   431

389 soote: sweet-smelling, fragrant
392 trench: path
393 glood: rose
394 rody: red
401 knotte: gist, main point
404 savour: taste
409 for drye: very dry (or because of dryness)
413 resouned of: resounded with
416 endelong: down the length of
417 shrighte: shrieked
418 prighte: stabbed
428 faucon peregryn: peregrine falcon
429 fremde: foreign
430 now and now: every now and then

An extract from The Squire's Tale in Chaucer's *Canterbury Tales*

Words from Latin and Greek

When the Normans conquered Britain at the Battle of Hastings in 1066 they brought with them a form of French that became the official language of the court and gradually infiltrated the language of general use, producing a form that is called Middle English. The ultimate sources of these words were Latin and Greek, and in English many of them are more formal in use, like *commence* and *purchase*. Words of this kind often survive alongside older words derived from Anglo-Saxon which are used in everyday English, like *begin* and *buy*.

Many of these words are spelt in a way that is close to the original forms, and this accounts for the strange appearance of words like *castle*, *column*, and *foreign*.

The spread of the Norman language affected the spelling of existing English words too: *queen*, for example, is the Norman spelling of a word that in Anglo-Saxon was spelt *cwen*.

Words from other languages

In more recent times, English has borrowed words from many other languages. Some of these words have changed their form to look like English words: for example *cockroach* from Spanish *cucaracha*. Others have retained their original spelling: for example *gnu* (from an African language, pronounced noo) and *karate* (from Japanese, pronounced ka-**rah**-ti).

The effect of printing on spelling

A stable spelling system is relatively recent. Before the invention of printing in the fifteenth century, it was common to spell words, and even people's names, according to individual choice. The word *world*, for example, is first recorded in the forms *weorold* and *wuruld*, and went through various forms such as *weorld* and *wordle*, as well as several northern and Scottish spellings including *warld* and *wardle*, before developing the more recognizable form that we know today. In fact, the *Oxford English Dictionary* lists over fifty spellings divided into five groups! Some of the early printers, who came from abroad, applied to English words practices they took from other languages; this explains the *h* in *ghost* (which was influenced by the Flemish word *gheest*) and the *p* in *receipt* (which was influenced by the medieval Latin word *recepta*).

> **world** (wɜːld), *sb.* Forms: α. 1 weorold, wuruld, worold, uoruld, wiarald, 1–3 weoruld, woruld, -eld, -old, 2 wurold, 3 we(o)reld, wæruld, *Orm.* we(o)relld. β. 1– world; 1–3 weorld, 4–6 worlde (2 worlð, 3 wurld, 5 whorlld(e); 2–3 werlð, 3 *Orm.* werrld, 3–5 werld(e; *north.* and *Sc.* 3– warld, 5–6 warlde, varld, (5 warlede). γ. 4–6 wordle, 5 wordel, wordil; *north.* and *Sc.* 5–7 wardle, 6 wardill, vardil, wardel, vardel; 3 werdle. δ. 3–6 word, 4–5 worde (6 woaude); 3–5 werd, 4–5 werde; 4 wird; *north.* 4, 6 ward. ε. 3 worl, 3–5 worle, 5 worlle, orlle, 6 worell; 8 worl', *north.* and *Sc.* 5 warle, 8 warl', 9 warl. [Com. Teut. (wanting in Gothic): OE. *weorold, worold, world* str. f., rarely m., corresp. to OFris. *wrald, ruald, warld* (EFris. *warld*, WFris. *wrôd*), OS. *werold* (MLG. *werlt, warlt*, LG. *werld*, MDu. *werelt*, Du. *wereld*), OHG. *weralt* (MHG. *werelt, werlt, welt*, G. *welt*), ON. *veröld* (Sw. *verld*, Da. *verden*): a formation peculiar to Germanic, f. *wer-* man, WERE *sb.*[1] + *ald-* age (cf. OLD *a.*, ELD

From the entry for *world* in the *Oxford English Dictionary*

People spelt the same words differently because consistency was not regarded as important, and because with the spread of literacy many more people were writing. More of the vernacular or common language was being written, and individuals used their own method of spelling. There was no attempt to standardize spelling because there was no need to: as long as people could understand what you had written there didn't seem to be a problem.

Ideas for spelling reform

There have been many proposals over the years for changing the way we spell words, and there are people today who believe that a reform would make spelling easier and more logical and communication more effective as a result.

Benjamin Franklin and Bernard Shaw

In 1768, the American statesman Benjamin Franklin (who was also a printer and publisher) devised an alphabet that dispensed with the letters *c, j, q, w, x,* and *y,* which he considered unnecessary because other letters could be used for the same sounds. Most other attempts at reform have concentrated on producing a larger number of letters so that complications such as digraphs (two letters pronounced as one) could be eliminated. These include proposals in the 19th century by Isaac Pitman, the inventor of shorthand, and in the 20th century by George Bernard Shaw, who donated money to fund a competition to design a new alphabet.

A phonetic alphabet?

In particular, people have suggested devising a system in which each sound has its own letter, so that every word would be spelt as it sounds and words that are pronounced the same way would be spelt the same way.

Not as easy as it sounds

One difficulty with this principle, attractive though it seems on the face of it, is that the same word can be pronounced differently in different parts of the British Isles (not to mention abroad); which system of pronunciation would be chosen as the basis? And even if this could be decided, a particular word is not always pronounced the same way in different contexts.

For example, the word *the* can be pronounced like *thee, ther,* or *thi* according to what follows (*thee apple, ther book, in thi afternoon*). *Have* is pronounced in one way in the sentence *Have you seen him?* and in another way in the sentence *I could have seen him.* In the first sentence *have* has a full *a* sound like the one in *hat*, whereas in the second sentence it is a much shorter sound more like the *e* in *garden.*

There's another problem: words that sound the same but are distinguished by their spelling, like *pair* and *pear*, and *loan* and *lone*, not to mention *there*, *their*, and *they're*, would all be spelt the same way, and we would not be able to distinguish them. This might not always matter, but it could be very confusing, because the spelling of a word often provides a clue about what it means. It would make reading, where these clues are important, very much more difficult.

There!
It's their cats.
They're drunk again.

A phonetic alphabet may not be a good idea

Some words are pronounced differently in different grammatical roles. For example, *record* has a stress (emphasis) on the first syllable *rec-* when it is a noun (as in *a record*) and on the second syllable *-cord* when it is a verb (as in *to record*), and the *e* sound is different. There are many others like this, such as *conflict*, *decrease*, *insult*, and *suspect*. In each case, the noun and the verb would have to be spelt differently, even though they are the same word. The connection between the noun *house*, in which the *s* is pronounced as in *hiss*, and the verb (*to*) *house*, in which it is pronounced like a *z*, would be obscured. And words that are related in origin would lose their written link altogether if they were spelt as they were pronounced, because related words often change their pronunciation (as with *sign* and *signal*, and *line* and *linear*).

5 Looking back : how
spelling got to be
so difficult

Not the answer

In short, a phonetic spelling system would destroy the frame-
work on which our reading and understanding of words and
their relationships depend. We might be able to spell more
easily, but the value of the words that we spelt in this way
would be greatly reduced.

Who is to say?

Quite apart from all these objections to a reformed alphabet,
there is no authoritative body for English that is in any position
to impose such as change on the language. So we are stuck
with the present system, warts and all.

Part B
Quick Reference

This section gives you information about different types of spelling difficulty in the form of lists, with explanations when needed. Use this section to check on particular problems and to get extra information to help you with the strategies explained in the first part of the book.

Contents of this section

How to find your word in this section

A list of the main topics to do with spelling is given below.

The arrows (➤) after each topic refer you to the numbered headings and subheadings in this section. Numbers of main headings are in bold type (e.g. **1**). Numbers of subheadings (if any) are in the form 1.1, 1.2, etc

Is it a word that's just awkward? ➤ **1**

    a short word like *eighth* or *seize*? ➤ 1.1

    a long word with a lot of awkward letters? ➤ 1.2

Is it a word that you can easily confuse with another one?

    like *pear* and *pair*? ➤ **2**

    like *practice* and *practise*? ➤ **3**

Is it a word with different possible spellings? ➤ **4**

    Is it a choice between -*able* and -*ible*? ➤ 4.1
             between -*acy* and -*asy*? ➤ 4.2
             between -*ance* and -*ence* or -*ancy* and -*ency*? ➤ 4.3
             between -*ant* and -*ent*? ➤ 4.4
             between -*ary*, -*ery*, and -*ory*? ➤ 4.5
             between -*cede*, -*ceed*, and -*sede*? ➤ 4.6
             between -*ch* and -*tch*? ➤ 4.7
             between -*efy* and -*ify*? ➤ 4.8
             between -*ei*- and -*ie*-? ➤ 4.9
             between -*er* and -*or*? ➤ 4.10
             between -*ious* and -*eous*? ➤ 4.11
             between -*ize* and -*ise*? ➤ 4.12
             between -*sion* and -*tion*? ➤ 4.13

Is it about whether to drop an *e* at the end, e.g. *guid(e)ance*, *blu(e)ish*? ➤ **5**

Is it a choice between single and double letters, e.g. *harass*, *accommodation*? ➤ **6**

1 Problem words

Some quite short words cause as much trouble as the long complicated ones. For example, *eighth*, *guard*, and *niece* are among the most commonly misspelt words in English and are only one syllable long.

1.1 Short words

Here is a list of troublesome short words:

chief	height	pierce	strength
eighth	juice	priest	twelfth
gauge	length	seize	weird
guard	niece	siege	yield

1.2 Long words

Most of the words that cause problems, however, are long ones. Here is a list of the words that cause most trouble:

abbreviation	aggressive	assassinate
abhorrence	aggression	asthma
accelerator	aghast	attach
accessory	allege	attachment
accommodate	allotment	attendant
accommodation	ambidextrous	autumn
accompaniment	annihilate	bankruptcy
achievement	annihilation	barbecue
acknowledgement	annul	baulk
acquaint	annulment	beautiful
acquaintance	anonymous	beginner
acquiesce	answer	beginning
acquire	apologize	behaviour
acquit	apostasy	belief
address	appalling	believe
adequate	apparently	beneficent
advantageous	arbitrary	berserk
advertise	archaeology	biased
advertisement	artefact	billionaire
aggravate	asphalt	biscuit

bourgeois
breathalyse
broccoli
budgeting
buoyant
bureaucracy
burglar
calendar (of dates)
camouflage
caress
carriage
cannabis
cassette
catalogue
catarrh
cauliflower
cemetery
chameleon
champagne
changeable
cigarette
coconut
collaborate
collapsible
colossal
commemorate
commiserate
commitment
committed
committee
comparative
compatible
compel
compelling
competent
conceive
conference
connection
connoisseur
conscientious
consensus
controversy

convalesce
convalescence
cooperate
cooperation
cooperative
copier
counterfeit
cupful
curriculum
cylinder
deceive
definite
dependant (noun)
dependent
  (adjective)
descendant
desiccated
desperate
detach
detachment
diaphragm
diarrhoea
diphtheria
diphthong
disappear
disappearance
disappoint
disappointed
disappointment
disapprove
dispatch (*despatch* is
  also correct)
dispel
dissect
dissipate
ecstasy
effervesce
efficient
eligible
embarrass
embarrassed
embarrassment

encyclopedia
  (*encyclopaedia* is
  also correct)
endeavour
enthral
enrol
enrolment
equipped
equipment
euthanasia
exaggerate
exasperate
exceed
excellent
excerpt
exercise
exhibition
exhilarate
extraordinary
extravagant
extrovert
fascinate
February
fetus (*foetus* is also
  correct)
fledgling (*fledgeling*
  is also correct)
fluorescent
foreign
foreigner
forfeit
fulfil
generation
ghastly
ghetto
giraffe
government
graffiti
grandad
granddaughter
grievous
guarantee

guaranteed
guardian
guillotine
gymnastics
gypsy
haemorrhage
hallucination
handful
handicap
handkerchief
harass
harassed
harassment
hereditary
honorary
honourable
humorous
hygiene
hygienic
hypochondriac
hypocrisy
idiosyncrasy
illegitimate
illiterate
impostor
inadvertent
inconceivable
independent
   (adjective and
   noun)
indispensable
infallible
innocuous
inseparable
install
instalment
interrogate
interrogation
interrupt
interruption
invisible
irascible

irreplaceable
irresistible
irresponsible
irritable
jeopardize
jewellery (*jewelry* is
   also correct)
judgement
   (*judgment* is also
   correct)
keenness
khaki
kidnapper
kilometre
lackadaisical
lacquer
languor
latish (= fairly late)
lecherous
leisure
leopard
liaise
liaison
library
lieutenant
liquefy
literature
luscious
macabre
macaroon
magnanimous
maintenance
manageable
manoeuvre
marijuana
marmalade
marriage
martyr
marvellous
massacre
mayonnaise
medicine

medieval
mellifluous
memento
mileage (*milage* is
   also correct)
millennium
millionaire
miniature
minuscule
miscellaneous
mischievous
misshapen
misspell
moccasin
mortgage
moustache
mouthful
Muhammad
naive (*naïve* is
   also correct)
necessary
negligent
negligible
noticeable
nuisance
obscene
occasionally
occurrence
omelette
omission
omit
omitted
opponent
paediatric
paedophile
paraffin
parliament
parallel
paralleled
perceive
permanent
perseverance

persevere
pharaoh
pigeon
plausible
Portuguese
precede
preceding
preferable
prejudice
prerogative
proceed
pronunciation
pseudonym
psychology
pygmy
pyjamas
pyramid
quarrelsome
questionnaire
queuing
rarefy
receipt
receive
recommend
reconnaissance
redundant
refrigerator
regrettable
relieve
reminiscence
remittance
reservoir
responsible
restaurant
restaurateur
resuscitate
rheumatism
rhythm

Romanian
sacrilege
sacrilegious
sandwich
sausage
scavenge
schizophrenia
secretary
separate
sergeant (military)
Shakespeare
shepherd
signature
silhouette
simultaneous
skilful
solemn
somersault
sovereign
spaghetti
spoonful
steadfast
subtle
subtlety
subtly
successful
suddenness
superintendent
supersede
supplement
suppress
surveillance
susceptible
sustenance
synagogue
syringe
targeted
tariff

tattoo
temperament
temperamental
temperature
temporarily
temporary
terrible
thinness
threshold
toffee
tranquillity
transferable
traveller
treacherous
tremor
typical
unconscious
unconstitutional
unforgettable
unforgivable
ungrammatical
unnecessary
unwieldy
vacuum
vegetable
vehicle
vengeance
veterinary
Wednesday
whether
wholly
withhold
woollen
woolly
worshipper
yoghurt (*yogurt* is
    also correct)
zoology

2 Confusable spellings

Some words are misspelt because they are like other words and are often confused with them. Here is a list of words that are most often confused in this way.

aboard	(on a ship or aircraft)	abroad	(in a foreign country)
accept	(to take)	except	(apart from)
affect	(to make a difference to)	effect	(something caused; to bring about)
aisle	(in a church or theatre)	isle	(island)
allude	(to refer to)	elude	(to escape from)
allusion	(reference)	illusion	(false appearance)
altar	(in a church)	alter	(to change)
angel	(holy being)	angle	(between two lines)
annex	(verb)	annexe	(noun)
arc	(part of curve)	ark	(ship)
ascent	(going up)	assent	(agreement)
aural	(to do with hearing)	oral	(using speech)
bail	(payment to secure release; and as in *bail someone out*)	bale	(of hay; and as in *bale out* of an aircraft)
bare	(naked)	bear	(to carry; animal)
base	(lowest part, etc)	bass	(low singing voice)
bazaar	(covered market)	bizarre	(strange)
beach	(by the sea)	beech	(tree)
bean	(edible seed)	been	(past participle of *be*)
beat	(to hit, etc)	beet	(vegetable)
beer	(drink)	bier	(stand for coffin)
berry	(round growth on bush)	bury	(to put in the ground)

berth	(for ship)	birth	(being born)		
blew	(past of *blow*)	blue	(colour)		
blond	(male person)	blonde	(female person)		
boar	(a wild pig)	boor	(an ill-mannered person)	bore	(a dull person or task
born ·	(as in *she was born on a Sunday*)	borne	(as in *she has borne a lot of troubles*)		
bough	of tree)	bow	(as in *take a bow*)		
boy	(male child)	buoy	(floating in sea)		
brake	(for stopping)	break	(to come to pieces, etc)		
breach	(to break through)	breech	(part of gun, etc)		
breath	(noun)	breathe	(verb)		
bridal	(of a bride)	bridle	(of a horse)		
broach	(to mention)	brooch	(ornament)		
buy	(to purchase)	by	(as in *by the way*)	bye	(in cricket)
cache	(hidden store)	cash	(money)		
cannon	(large gun)	canon	(church and music senses)		
canvas	(coarse cloth)	canvass	(seek vote, etc)		
carat	(of gold)	carrot	(vegetable)		
cast	(to throw, actors in film, etc)	caste	(as in *caste system*)		
caster	(sugar)	castor	(swivelling wheel; oil)		
ceiling	(of room)	sealing	(closing)		
cell	(small room)	sell	(to give for money)		
censor	(an official who rates films)	censure	(to express disapproval of)		

cent	(money)	scent	(perfume)	sent	(past and past participle of *send*)
cereal	(food)	serial	(on television, etc)		
cheap	(not expensive)	cheep	(bird's sound)		
check	(to verify, etc)	cheque	(for paying money)		
chilli	(food)	chilly	(cold)		
choir	(singing)	quire	(of paper)		
chord	(group of notes)	cord	(string or rope, *spinal cord*, etc)		
chute	(for sliding down)	shoot	(to fire a gun, etc)		
cite	(to name or mention)	sight	(vision)	site	(as in *building site*)
coarse	(rough, crude)	course	(as in *French course*, *racecourse*, etc)		
complacent	(too easily satisfied)	complaisant	(liking to please other people)		
complement	(extra thing)	compliment	(expression of praise)		
corps	(a group of people, as in *diplomatic corps*)	corpse	(a dead body)		
council	(official body)	counsel	(advice, lawyer in court)		
councillor	(member of council)	counsellor	(adviser)		
courtesy	(politeness)	curtsy	(formal greeting)		
creak	(to make noise)	creek	(waterway)		
crochet	(handicraft)	crotchet	(in music)		

cue	(signal)	queue	(line of people)
curb	(a restraint)	kerb	(of pavement)
currant	(dried fruit)	current	(of water, etc; happening now)
cygnet	(young swan)	signet	(ring)
cymbal	(in music)	symbol	(sign)
dairy	(a place that produces milk etc.)	diary	(a book for writing details for each day)
dam	(barrier)	damn	(to condemn)
dear	(expensive; beloved)	deer	(animal)
defuse	(take fuse from)	diffuse	(widely spread)
dependant	(noun in British English)	dependent	(adjective, also noun in American English)
desert	(to abandon, waterless place)	dessert	(sweet course)
device	(noun, something you use)	devise	(verb, as in *to devise a plan*)
dew	(morning wetness)	due	(as in *due to*)
die	(to suffer death)	dye	(to colour)
dinghy	(small boat)	dingy	(gloomy)
discreet	(careful and cautious)	discrete	(separate, distinct)
discus	(for throwing)	discuss	(to talk about)
doe	(female deer)	dough	(flour mixture)
draft	(first version)	draught	(current of air, type of beer, etc.)
dual	(double)	duel	(fight)
dyeing	(from *dye*)	dying	(from *die*)
eerie	(strange and scary)	eyrie	(large high nest)
elicit	(to draw out information)	illicit	(not lawful)

eligible	(satisfying conditions)	illegible	(not readable)		
ensure	(to make sure)	insure	(to take out insurance on)		
envelop	(verb)	envelope	(noun)		
ewe	(female sheep)	yew	(tree)	you	(personal pronoun)
exercise	(physical activity)	exorcise	(to drive out a spirit)		
faint	(barely perceptible)	feint	(pretended attack, and of lined paper)		
fair	(just, place for amusement)	fare	(charge for journey, etc)		
fate	(destiny)	fête	(outdoor function)		
feat	(achievement)	feet	(plural of *foot*)		
ferment	(of alcohol, unrest, to cause unrest)	foment	(to stir up strife)		
fir	(tree)	fur	(of animal)		
flair	(special talent)	flare	(bright flame)		
flea	(insect)	flee	(to escape)		
flew	(past of fly)	flu	(illness)	flue	(pipe or passage)
floe	(a sheet of floating ice)	flow	(as in *a flowing river*)		
flour	(powder from grain)	flower	(part of plant)		
for	(as in *a room for eating*)	fore	(as in *to the fore*)	four	(number)
forebear	(ancestor)	forbear	(to refrain)		
forego	(to go before)	forgo	(to go without)		
forth	(as in *go forth*)	fourth	(as in *fourth place*)		
forward	(as in *move forward*)	foreword	(of book)		

foul	(dirty)	fowl	(bird)			
franc	(French currency)	frank	(honest)			
freeze	(to make cold)	frieze	(decorated band on wall)			
gait	(manner of walking)	gate	(entrance to field ,etc)			
gamble	(to play games of chance)	gambol	(to jump about)			
gaol	(prison)	goal	(objective)			
gild	(cover with gold)	guild	(association)			
gilt	(covered with gold)	guilt	(feeling)			
gorilla	(animal)	guerrilla	(fighter)			
grate	(to make into small shreds, fireplace)	great	(large, important, etc)			
grill	(in cooking)	grille	(set of metal bars)			
grisly	(horrible)	gristly	(meat)	grizzly	(bear)	
hail	(to call out to, frozen rain)	hale	(as in *hale and hearty*)			
hair	(on head)	hare	(animal)			
hangar	(large shed)	hanger	(for hanging clothes)			
hart	(male deer)	heart	(organ)			
heal	(to cure)	heel	(of foot)			
hear	(to perceive sound)	here				
heroin	(drug)	heroine	(female hero)			
hew	(to cut down)	hue	(shade)			
higher	(more high)	hire	(as in *hire a car*)			
him	(from *he*)	hymn	(singing)			
hoar	(frost)	whore	(prostitute)			
hoard	(large secret supply)	horde	(crowd of people)			

hoarse	(sore in throat)	horse	(animal)		
hole	(opening)	whole	(entire)		
hoop	(round thing)	whoop	(joyful cry)		
idle	(inactive)	idol	(object of worship)		
in	(as in *come in*, *in the bath*)	inn	(small hotel)		
interment	(burial)	internment	(imprisonment)		
its	(as in *the cat licked its paws*)	it's	(as in *it's raining*, *it's been raining*)		
jam	(food, traffic)	jamb	(of door)		
key	(to open door)	quay	(for ships)		
knave	(villain)	nave	(of church)		
knead	(to work dough)	kneed	(hit with the knee)	need	(to require, necessity)
knew	(past of *know*)	new	(as in *a new car*)		
knight	(in armour)	night	(time after sunset)		
knit	(use wool)	nit	(insect)		
knot	(in rope, speed)	not	(negative word)		
know	(to have knowledge)	no	(negative word)		
lain	(past participle of *lie*)	lane	(narrow road)		
lair	(of animal)	layer	(as in *layer of icing*)		
lama	(Buddhist monk)	llama	(animal)		
lea	(grassy land)	lee	(shelter from wind)		
lead	(metal)	led	(past and past participle of *lead*)		
leak	(escape of liquid, etc)	leek	(vegetable)		

lessen	(to reduce)	lesson	(as in *maths lesson*)
liar	(someone who tells lies)	lyre	(musical instrument)
licence	(noun)	license	(verb)
lightening	(making lighter)	lightning	(in sky)
liqueur	(an alcoholic drink)	liquor	(alcoholic drinks generally)
literal	(as in *the literal truth*)	littoral	(region near the shore of a sea)
load	(amount carried)	lode	(vein of metal)
loan	(money lent)	lone	(solitary)
loath or loth	(as in *loath to admit it*)	loathe	(to detest)
loose	(not well fixed, to make loose)	lose	(to suffer the loss of)
loot	(property taken in war)	lute	(musical instrument)
lumbar	(lower back)	lumber	(unwanted furniture etc.)
made	(past and past participle of make)	maid	(female servant)
magnate	(wealthy person)	magnet	(object that attracts metal)
mail	(letters etc., armour)	male	(sex)
main	(chief)	mane	(of horse etc.)
maize	(cereal)	maze	(puzzle)
manner	(way or bearing)	manor	(country house)
mare	(female horse)	mayor	(head of city)
marshal	(law officer)	martial	(of war)
mat	(floor covering)	matt	(dull finish)
medal	(as in *gold medal*)	meddle	(to interfere)

meat	(flesh)	meet	(to encounter)	mete	(as in *to mete out punishment* etc.)
metal	(solid material)	mettle	(as in *be on one's mettle*)		
meter	(gauge or measure)	metre	(unit of length)		
mews	(row of houses)	muse	(goddess)		
might	(power)	mite	(insect)		
miner	(worker in mines)	minor	(having little importance; in music)		
moat	(water round walls)	mote	(a speck)		
moose	(large animal)	mouse	(rodent)	mousse	(foamy stuff)
muscle	(body tissue)	mussel	(mollusc)		
naught	(as in *set at naught*)	nought	(zero)		
naval	(to do with a navy or ships)	navel	(orange; belly button)		
oar	(for rowing)	ore	(containing metal)	or	(as in *either … or …*)
of	(as in *a packet of seeds*)	off	(as in *take off, off the mark*)		
pail	(bucket)	pale	(light in shade)		
pain	(unpleasant feeling)	pane	(of glass)		
pair	(set of two)	pare	(to cut or trim)	pear	(fruit)
palate	(roof of mouth)	palette	(board for colours)	pallet	(storage platform)
passed	(as in *Three cars passed us*)	past	(as in *We went past them*)		
pastel	(pale shade)	pastille	(sweet or lozenge)		

peace	(freedom from war)	piece	(portion)		
peak	(tip, highest point, etc.)	peek	(to look furtively)	pique	(spiteful resentment)
peal	(of bells)	peel	(skin of fruit)		
pedal	(of bicycle etc)	peddle	(to sell)		
peer	(person of same age; member of nobility; to look keenly)	pier	(platform at seaside)		
pendant	(piece of jewellery	pendent	(hanging)		
personal	(private)	personnel	(people employed)		
petrel	(seabird)	petrol	(fuel)		
pistil	(of flower)	pistol	(gun)		
place	(location)	plaice	(fish)		
plain	(level ground, undecorated)	plane	(flat surface, aeroplane, tree)		
plum	(fruit)	plumb	(measure depth of water, fit plumbing)		
pore	(as in *pore over books*, opening in skin)	pour	(as in *to pour tea*)		
practice	(noun)	practise	(verb)		
pray	(to say prayers)	prey	(hunted animal)		
principal	(chief, main)	principle	(a truth or rule)		
prise	(as in *to prise open*)	prize	(to value highly)		
profit	(gain)	prophet	(someone who predicts future)		
program	(in computing)	programme	(in general meanings)		

prophecy	(noun)	prophesy	(verb)
put	(in general meanings)	putt	(in golf)
rain	(weather)	reign	(to rule as king or queen)	rein (for horse; to confine)
raise	(to lift up)	raze	(to destroy buildings)
rest	(to relax)	wrest	(take forcibly)
retch	(to vomit)	wretch	(unfortunate person)
review	(survey or assessment	revue	(entertainment) etc.)
rhyme	(in poetry)	rime	(frost)
right	(correct, opposite to *left*, an entitlement)	rite	(ritual)	write (put down words)
ring	(make sound of bell, thing worn on finger, etc.)	wring	(squeeze water from)
road	(way for travelling)	rode	(past of *ride*)	rowed (past and past participle of *row*)
roe	(small deer, fish eggs)	row	(series in line)
role	(function)	roll	(to turn over and over, act of rolling, etc.)
rote	(as in *learn by rote*)	wrote	(past of *write*)
rough	(not smooth, violent)	ruff	(starched frill)
rout	(disorderly retreat or defeat)	route	(way or course)

rung	(part of ladder, past participle of *ring*)	wrung	(past participle of *wring*)		
rye	(cereal, whisky)	wry	(drily humorous)		
sail	(of a boat)	sale	(selling of goods)		
scene	(view etc.)	seen	(past participle of *see*)		
sceptic	(cautiously doubtful)	septic	(infected)		
sea	(ocean)	see	(to perceive with the eyes, seat of a bishop)		
seam	(join in fabric etc.)	seem	(to appear)		
sear	(to burn)	seer	(prophet)		
sew	(with needle etc.)	so	(as in *not so bad*)	sow	(seed)
shear	(to cut wool etc.)	sheer	(as in *sheer delight*, *a sheer drop*)		
shoe	(for feet)	shoo	(to send away)		
singeing	(from *singe*)	singing	(from *sing*)		
slay	(to kill)	sleigh	(sledge)		
sloe	(fruit)	slow	(not fast)		
soar	(rise high)	sore	(painful)		
sole	(one and only,	soul	(spirit) underside of foot, fish)		
some	(as in *have some cake*)	sum	(amount of money etc.)		
son	(male child)	sun	(star)		
soot	(black powder)	suit	(of clothes; of cards)	suite	(of rooms or furniture; in music)
staid	(respectable)	stayed	(past and past participle of *stay*)		

stair	(step)	stare	(to gaze)
stake	(post, money bet)	steak	(meat)
stationary	(not moving)	stationery	(paper etc.)
steal	(to take without right)	steel	(metal, and in *to steel oneself*)
step	(movement in walking etc.)	steppe	(area of grassland)
stile	(for getting over fence)	style	(distinctive manner etc.)
storey	(of building)	story	(tale)
straight	(without curve)	strait	(passage of water)
straightened	(made straight)	straitened	(restricted)
suite	(of rooms or furniture; in music)	sweet	(of taste)
summary	(short version)	summery	(like summer)
sundae	(food)	Sunday	(day of week)
surplice	(church vestment)	surplus	(extra amount)
swingeing	(severe)	swinging	(from *swing*)
tail	(of animal)	tale	(story)
taper	(to narrow)	tapir	(animal)
tare	(plant, weight)	tear	(to rip, to rush)
taught	(past and past participle of teach)	taut	(pulled tight)
tea	(drink)	tee	(in golf)
team	(group of players)	teem	(to swarm; to rain heavily)
tear	(from eyes)	tier	(row or level)
teeth	(plural of tooth)	teethe	(to cut new teeth)
tenor	(singing voice)	tenure	(right to hold office or land)

their	(as in *their house*)	there	(as in *the house over there*)	they're	(as in *they're moving house*)
thrash	(to beat)	thresh	(to separate grain)
threw	(past of *throw*)	through	(as in *go through, through the window*)
throes	(as in *in the throes of*)	throws	(from *throw*)
thyme	(herb)	time	(past, present, future)
tic	(spasm)	tick	(of clock etc., mark)
tire	(to become tired)	tyre	(on wheel)
to	(as in *the road to London*)	too	(as in *I want one too, not too much*)	two	(number)
toe	(part of foot, and in *toe the line*)	tow	(to pull)
ton	(non-metric weight)	tonne	(metric weight)	tun	(cask or vat)
trait	(characteristic)	tray	(for putting things on)
troop	(group of soldiers)	troupe	(group of performers)
turban	(headdress)	turbine	(machine)
vain	(conceited, and in *in vain*)	vane	(as in *weather vane*)	vein	(carrying blood)
vale	(valley)	veil	(worn over face)
veracity	(truth)	voracity	(greed)
waive	(to decline a right)	wave	(to signal, movement in water)
waist	(middle of body)	waste	(rubbish, to use badly)

ware	(articles)	wear	(clothing)		
way	(manner, route)	weigh	(to find weight of)		
weak	(not strong)	week .	(seven days)		
weather	(as in *fine weather*)	whether	(as in *I don't know whether they're coming*)		
wet	(affected by liquid)	whet	(as in *whet one's appetite*)		
whit	(as in *not a whit*)	wit	(intelligence, humour)		
who's	(= *who is, who has*)	whose	(as in *whose book is this?*)		
wood	(from trees)	would	(verb)		
wreath	(arrangement of leaves etc.)	wreathe	(to encircle)		
yoke	(wooden crosspiece or frame)	yolk	(of egg)		
yore	(as in *days of yore*)	your	(as in *your book*)	you're	(= *you are*)

3 Spelling differences between related nouns and verbs

Sometimes words with slightly different spellings are used in related meanings of nouns and verbs, for example *practice* (with a *c*) is a noun and *practise* (with an *s*) is a verb.

Here is a list of the most common of these:

Noun	Verb
advice	advise
bath	bathe
belief	believe
breath	breathe
calf	calve
cloth	clothe
grief	grieve
half	halve
licence	license
practice	practise
prophecy	prophesy
relief	relieve
sheath	sheathe
shelf	shelve
teeth	teethe
thief	thieve

4 Choosing from alternatives

4.1 Adjectives ending in -*able* and -*ible*

-*able*

abominable
actionable
adaptable
administrable
admittable
  (*also* admissible)
adorable
advisable
agreeable
alienable
amenable
amiable
analysable
appreciable
arguable
ascribable
assessable
atonable
available
bearable
believable
blameable
bribable
bridgeable
calculable
capable
changeable
chargeable
clubbable
collectable
comfortable
conceivable
conferrable
confinable
consolable
contractable

(*of a disease; see
also* contractible)
copiable
creatable
curable
datable
debatable
declinable
defendable
  (*in literal meanings;
see also
defensible*)
deferable
definable
delineable
demonstrable
demurrable
deniable
desirable
despicable
developable
dilatable
dispensable
disposable
dissolvable
drivable
durable
dutiable
eatable
educable (= *able to
be educated;
see also* educible)
endorsable
equable
evadable
excisable

excitable
excusable
expandable
  (*also* expansible)
expendable
expiable
extendable
  (*also* extendible,
extensible)
feeable
finable
foreseeable
forgettable
forgivable
framable
gettable
giveable
hireable
illimitable
immovable
immutable
impalpable
impassable
  (= *unable to be
crossed; see also*
impassible)
impeccable
imperturbable
implacable
impressionable
improvable
indefatigable
indescribable
indispensable
indubitable
inflatable

inimitable
insufferable
irreconcilable
irreplaceable
justifiable
knowledgeable
laughable
leviable
likeable
liveable
losable
lovable
machinable
malleable
manageable
manoeuvrable
marriageable
measurable
mistakable
movable
mutable
nameable
noticeable
objectionable
obtainable

operable
palatable
payable
peaceable
penetrable
perishable
permeable
persuadable
    (*also* persuasible)
pleasurable
preferable
prescribable
preventable
pronounceable
provable
rateable
readable
receivable
reconcilable
rectifiable
registrable
regrettable
reliable
removable
reputable

retractable
saleable
scalable
serviceable
sizeable
solvable
statutable
storable
suitable
superannuable
timeable
tolerable
traceable
tradable
transferable
tuneable
unconscionable
undeniable
unexceptionable
unget-at-able
unknowable
unmistakable
unscalable
unshakeable
usable

-ible

accessible
adducible
admissible
    (*also* admittable)
audible
avertible
collapsible
comprehensible
contemptible
contractible (= *able
    to be shrunk*; *see
    also* contractable)
convertible
deducible

deductible
defensible
    (*of an argument
    etc.*; *see also*
    defendable)
destructible
diffusible
digestible
dirigible
discernible
discussible
dismissible
divisible
educible (= *able to be*

educed; *see also*
    educable)
eligible
exhaustible
expansible
expressible
extendible (*also*
    extendable,
    extensible)
feasible
flexible
fusible
gullible
illegible

impassible
(= *unfeeling*; *see also* impassable)
inaudible
incorrigible
incredible
indelible
indigestible
indivisible
infallible
inflexible
intangible
invincible

invisible
irascible
irreducible
irrepressible
irresponsible
irresistible
irreversible
legible
negligible
ostensible
perceptible
perfectible
permissible

persuasible (*also* persuadable)
plausible
reprehensible
reproducible
resistible
responsible
reversible
risible
suggestible
suppressible
susceptible
visible

4.2 Nouns in -*acy* and -*asy*

Most nouns of this type end in -*acy*:

accuracy
adequacy
advocacy
aristocracy
bureaucracy
candidacy
celibacy
confederacy
conspiracy
delicacy

democracy
diplomacy
efficacy
fallacy
immediacy
intimacy
intricacy
legacy
legitimacy
literacy

lunacy
magistracy
numeracy
obstinacy
papacy
pharmacy
privacy
profligacy
supremacy
surrogacy

There are only four commonly used nouns that end in -*asy*:

apostasy
ecstasy
fantasy
idiosyncrasy

4.3 Nouns ending in -*ance* and -*ence*

-*ance*

aberrance
abeyance
acceptance
accordance
acquaintance
admittance
allegiance
alliance
allowance
ambulance
annoyance
appearance
appliance
appurtenance
arrogance
assistance
assurance
attendance
avoidance
balance
brilliance
capacitance
circumstance
clairvoyance
clearance
cognizance
come-uppance
complaisance
compliance
concordance
connivance
continuance
contrivance
conveyance
countenance
defiance
deliverance
deviance

disappearance
discordance
distance
disturbance
dominance
elegance
encumbrance
endurance
exorbitance
extravagance
exuberance
flamboyance
forbearance
fragrance
furtherance
governance
grievance
guidance
happenstance
hindrance
ignorance
imbalance
importance
inductance
inheritance
insouciance
instance
insurance
intemperance
intolerance
irrelevance
luminance
luxuriance
maintenance
malfeasance
misalliance
nonchalance
nuisance

observance
parlance
performance
perseverance
petulance
predominance
preponderance
protuberance
provenance
pursuance
radiance
reassurance
recalcitrance
recognizance
reconnaissance
relevance
reluctance
remembrance
remittance
remonstrance
repentance
repugnance
resemblance
resistance
resonance
riddance
semblance
significance
substance
sufferance
surveillance
sustenance
temperance
tolerance
utterance
variance
vengeance
vigilance

-ence

abhorrence	deterrence	incoherence
absence	difference	incompetence
abstinence	diffidence	incontinence
accidence	diligence	inconvenience
acquiescence	disobedience	independence
adherence	dissidence	indifference
adolescence	divergence	indigence
affluence	ebullience	indolence
ambience	effervescence	indulgence
ambivalence	efflorescence	inexpedience
antecedence	effluence	inexperience
audience	eloquence	inference
audience	emergence	inflorescence
belligerence	eminence	influence
beneficence	equivalence	innocence
benevolence	essence	insistence
circumference	evanescence	insolence
coexistence	evidence	insurgence
coherence	excellence	intelligence
coincidence	excrescence	interference
competence	existence	intransigence
concupiscence	expedience	iridescence
concurrence	experience	irreverence
condolence	flatulence	jurisprudence
conference	fluorescence	lenience
confidence	fraudulence	licence
confluence	grandiloquence	luminescence
congruence	imminence	magnificence
conscience	impatience	magniloquence
consequence	impenitence	malevolence
continence	impermanence	mellifluence
convalescence	impertinence	munificence
convenience	impotence	negligence
corpulence	improvidence	obedience
correspondence	imprudence	obsolescence
credence	impudence	occurrence
decadence	inadvertence	omnipotence
deference	incandescence	omnipresence
deliquescence	incidence	omniscience
dependence	incipience	opalescence

opulence
patience
penitence
percipience
permanence
persistence
pertinence
pestilence
phosphorescence
precedence
preeminence
preference
prescience
presence
prevalence
prominence
providence
prudence

prurience
pubescence
putrescence
quiescence
quintessence
recrudescence
recumbence
recurrence
reference
reminiscence
residence
resilience
resplendence
resurgence
reticence
reverence
salience
senescence

sentence
sequence
silence
subservience
subsidence
subsistence
succulence
supereminence
transcendence
transference
transience
truculence
tumescence
turbulence
turgescence
vehemence
violence
virulence

Note the following nouns ending in -*ancy* and -*ency*:

-*ancy*

accountancy
ascendancy
blatancy
buoyancy
constancy
consultancy
discrepancy

expectancy
flagrancy
hesitancy
inconstancy
infancy
malignancy
militancy

occupancy
pregnancy
redundancy
tenancy
truancy
vacancy
vibrancy

-ency

agency	despondency	leniency
clemency	efficiency	potency
complacency	emergency	proficiency
consistency	fluency	pungency
constituency	frequency	stridency
contingency	inconsistency	stringency
currency	indecency	sufficiency
decency	inefficiency	tendency
deficiency	insolvency	transparency
delinquency	insufficiency	urgency
dependency	latency	valency

4.4 Adjectives ending in -ant and -ent

-ant

aberrant	expectant	predominant
adamant	extravagant	preponderant
arrogant	exuberant	protuberant
attendant	flamboyant	pursuant
blatant	fragrant	radiant
brilliant	gallant	recalcitrant
clairvoyant	hesitant	recognizant
cognizant	ignorant	redundant
combatant	important	relevant
complaisant	incessant	reluctant
compliant	instant	repentant
defiant	intolerant	repugnant
depressant	irrelevant	resistant
deviant	luxuriant	resonant
discordant	militant	significant
distant	nonchalant	tolerant
dominant	observant	triumphant
elegant	petulant	variant
exorbitant	pleasant	vigilant

Note the following nouns: *coolant, dependant, inhabitant, irritant*

-ent

abhorrent	efficient	indulgent
absorbent	eloquent	inefficient
acquiescent	emergent	inexpedient
adherent	eminent	innocent
adolescent	equivalent	insistent
affluent	evanescent	insolent
ambient	evident	insolvent
ambivalent	excellent	insufficient
antecedent	existent	insurgent
belligerent	expedient	intelligent
beneficent	fervent	intermittent
benevolent	flatulent	intransigent
coherent	fluorescent	iridescent
competent	fraudulent	irreverent
complacent	grandiloquent	lenient
concurrent	imminent	luminescent
confident	impatient	magnificent
congruent	impenitent	magniloquent
consistent	impermanent	malevolent
continent	impertinent	mellifluent
convalescent	impotent	munificent
convenient	improvident	negligent
corpulent	imprudent	non-existent
current	impudent	obedient
decadent	inadvertent	obsolescent
decent	incandescent	omnipotent
delinquent	incident	omnipresent
dependent	incipient	omniscient
despondent	incoherent	opalescent
deterrent	incompetent	opulent
different	inconsistent	patient
diffident	incontinent	penitent
diligent	inconvenient	percipient
disobedient	indecent	permanent
dissident	independent	persistent
divergent	indifferent	pertinent
ebullient	indigent	pestilent
effervescent	indolent	phosphorescent

85

precedent	recrudescent	subservient
preeminent	recumbent	succulent
prescient	recurrent	sufficient
present	reminiscent	transcendent
prevalent	repellent	transient
prominent	resident	translucent
provident	resilient	truculent
prudent	resplendent	tumescent
prurient	resurgent	turbulent
pubescent	reticent	turgescent
putrescent	reverent	urgent
quiescent	salient	vehement
quintessent	silent	violent
recent	stringent	virulent

Note the following nouns: *continent, correspondent, effluent, precedent, referent, superintendent.*

4.5 Words ending in -*ary*, -*ery*, and -*ory*

-ary

Words ending in -*ary* can be nouns (e.g. *anniversary*) or adjectives (e.g. *ordinary*) or both (e.g. *contemporary*).

adversary	documentary	legendary
ancillary	elementary	library
anniversary	estuary	literary
arbitrary	exemplary	mercenary
auxiliary	extraordinary	military
beneficiary	fragmentary	missionary
boundary	funerary	momentary
burglary	glossary	monetary
centenary	hereditary	mortuary
commentary	honorary	necessary
complimentary	imaginary	obituary
contemporary	incendiary	ordinary
contrary	inflationary	parliamentary
customary	intermediary	pecuniary
dictionary	involuntary	penitentiary
disciplinary	itinerary	plenary
discretionary	judiciary	precautionary

preliminary
primary
probationary
proprietary
quandary
reactionary
revolutionary
rosary
rotary
rudimentary

salary
salutary
sanctuary
sanitary
secondary
secretary
sedentary
seminary
solitary
stationary

statuary
subsidiary
summary
supplementary
temporary
tributary
vagary
visionary
voluntary
vocabulary

-ery

Most words ending in -ery are nouns (the only adjective in the list is *slippery*).

adultery
archery
artery
artillery
bakery
battery
bravery
brewery
butchery
celery
cemetery
crockery
cutlery
delivery
discovery

distillery
drudgery
effrontery
flattery
forgery
gallery
imagery
jewellery
lottery
machinery
mastery
misery
mockery
monastery
mystery

nursery
pottery
recovery
refinery
robbery
scenery
slavery
slippery
snobbery
soldiery
stationery
surgery
treachery
trickery
upholstery

-ory

These can be nouns (e.g. *history*) or adjectives (e.g. *cursory*).

accessory
admonitory
advisory
allegory
amatory
category

conciliatory
conservatory
contradictory
contributory
cursory
defamatory

depository
derisory
derogatory
desultory
dilatory
directory

dormitory	lavatory	purgatory
explanatory	mandatory	rectory
factory	memory	satisfactory
history	obligatory	sensory
illusory	observatory	signatory
inflammatory	oratory	territory
introductory	predatory	theory
inventory	preparatory	trajectory
laboratory	priory	transitory
laudatory	promontory	victory

4.6 Words ending in *-cede*, *-ceed*, and *-sede*

There are not many of these words, but they are often confused.

-cede	-ceed	-sede
accede	exceed	supersede
concede	proceed	
intercede	succeed	
precede		
succeed		
recede		
secede		

Most of them end in *-cede* and only *supersede* ends in *-sede* (so be careful with this one.)

Beware of confusing *precede* and *proceed*.

4.7 Words ending in -ch and -tch

These cause a lot of problems: for example, *dispatch* is spelt with a *t* whereas *detach* is not. There are a few rules (and some exceptions):

If the final -ch sound comes after a consonant (any letter other than *a, e, i, o, u,* including *r* whether or not you pronounce it), there is no *t*, e.g. *branch, filch, church.*

If the -ch sound follows a single-letter vowel (*a, e, i, o, u*) it is written -*tch*, e.g. *batch, fetch, stitch, botch, hutch* (but *poach, teach, touch,* etc., which have a double-letter vowel).

There are a few exceptions to this last rule, and it is best simply to learn them:

attach	enrich	ostrich	sandwich	such
detach	much	rich	spinach	which

4.8 Words ending in -*efy* and -*ify*

Most words of this type end in -*ify*:

amplify	classify	justify	signify
beautify	disqualify	notify	simplify
certify	electrify	purify	unify
clarify	falsify	quantify	verify

There are only four common words that end in -*efy*:

liquefy	putrefy	rarefy	stupefy

4.9 Words with -*ei*- and -*ie*- in the spelling

These are words in which -*ei*- and -*ie*- form a single sound, often -ee- as in *meet*

Words marked * are exceptions to the rule given on page 24 about '*i* before *e* except after *c* when pronounced -ee-'

Words with -*ei*- in the spelling:

abseil	conceit	deceit
beige	conceited	deceitful
caffeine*	conceive	deceive
ceiling	counterfeit*	deign

eiderdown
eight
eighth
either
Fahrenheit
foreign
foreigner
forfeit
freight
freighter
heifer
height
heir
heiress
heirloom

kaleidoscope
leisure
neigh
neighbour
neither
perceive
poltergeist
protein*
receipt
receive
reign
rein
reindeer
rottweiler
seismograph

seize*
seizure*
sheikh
skein
sleigh
sovereign
spontaneity
their
theirs
veil
vein
weigh
weight
weir
weird

Words with -*ie*- in the spelling:

achieve
achievement
apiece
belief
believe
besiege
brief
chief
diesel
field
fiend
friend
frieze
grief
grievance
grieve

grievous
handkerchief
hygiene
hygienic
interview
mantelpiece
masterpiece
mischief
mischievous
niece
piece
pierce
preview
priest
relief
relieve

reprieve
retrieval
retrieve
retriever
review
series
shield
shriek
siege
sieve
thief
unwieldy
view
viewer
wield
yield

4.10 Nouns ending in -er and -or

-er is freely used to form nouns for people and things that do something (*baker, builder, mixer, opener, usurper, worker*).

-er is also used in a few words that are not derived from verbs and mostly denote people (*foreigner, jeweller, lawyer, mariner, prisoner, sorcerer, treasurer, usurer*).

-or is used in the following words:

accelerator	decorator	mediator
actor	defector	narrator
administrator	depositor	navigator
ambassador	dictator	objector
ancestor	director	operator
arbitrator	distributor	oppressor
auditor	doctor	orator
author	duplicator	pastor
aviator	editor	perpetrator
bachelor	educator	persecutor
benefactor	elevator	predecessor
calculator	emperor	processor
captor	equator	professor
censor	escalator	projector
chancellor	excavator	proprietor
collaborator	executor	prosecutor
collector	governor	prospector
commentator	impostor	protector
competitor	incubator	radiator
conductor	indicator	rector
conqueror	inheritor	reflector
conspirator	inquisitor	refrigerator
constructor	inspector	resistor
contractor	inventor	sailor
contributor	investigator	senator
councillor	investor	solicitor
counsellor	jailor	spectator
creator	janitor	sponsor
creditor	legislator	successor
curator	major	suitor
debtor	mayor	supervisor

surveyor	tractor	vendor
survivor	traitor	ventilator
tailor	translator	victor
tenor	tremor	visitor

-ar is used in a few words for people that do something:

beggar   burglar   liar   pedlar

-ar is also used in a few other nouns:

altar	collar	nectar
bursar	dollar	pillar
calendar	grammar	registrar
caterpillar	guitar	scholar
cedar	hangar	vicar
cellar	mortar	vinegar

4.11 Adjectives ending in *-ious* and *-eous*

Most adjectives pronounced like glorious end in *-ious*:

abstemious	ignominious	previous
acrimonious	illustrious	punctilious
amphibious	impecunious	rebellious
ceremonious	industrious	religious
censorious	ingenious	salubrious
commodious	injurious	sanctimonious
conscientious	laborious	sententious
copious	luxurious	serious
curious	melodious	spurious
delirious	nefarious	studious
devious	notorious	supercilious
dubious	obvious	superstitious
glorious	odious	tedious
harmonious	perfidious	uproarious
hilarious	pretentious	victorious

But there are a few adjectives that end in -*eous*:

aqueous	extraneous	instantaneous
beauteous	farinaceous	miscellaneous
bounteous	gaseous	nauseous
consanguineous	gorgeous	piteous
contemporaneous	heterogeneous	plenteous
courteous	hideous	simultaneous
discourteous	homogeneous	spontaneous
erroneous	igneous	subcutaneous

4.12 Verbs ending in -*ize* and -*ise*

Many verbs can end in either -*ize* or -*ise*. The important point is to be consistent. The publishers of this book use -*ize*. The following list is only a selection from a huge range of words:

agonize	finalize	privatize
Americanize	idealize	realize
Anglicize	idolize	recognize
appetize	legalize	serialize
brutalize	maximize	socialize
civilize	minimize	specialize
colonize	modernize	standardize
criticize	penalize	symbolize
equalize	philosophize	vandalize

The following is a list of words that must be spelt with -*ise*. The reason is usually that the ending -*ise* is not a separate suffix but part of a longer word element, for example -*cise* (meaning 'cutting' as in *excise*), -*prise* (meaning 'taking', as in *surprise*), and -*vise* (meaning 'seeing', as in *supervise*).

Because of this rule, many people always choose -*ise* because it is never wrong (but note that the verb *prize* has to be spelt with a z because -*ize* is part of the stem of the word and not an ending).

advertise	circumcise	devise
advise	comprise	disguise
apprise	compromise	enfranchise
chastise	despise	excise

exercise	promise	surprise
improvise	revise	televise
incise	supervise	
prise (open)	surmise	

Note also: *enterprising*.

4.13 Words ending in *-sion* and *-tion*

There are some patterns with these spellings to help you decide which is right.

If the pronunciation is as in *division*, the spelling is *-sion*:

cohesion	derision	intrusion
collision	division	persuasion
collusion	erosion	provision
conclusion	evasion	revision
confusion	exclusion	seclusion
corrosion	explosion	supervision
decision	fusion	television
delusion	illusion	vision

If the pronunciation is as in *condition*, the spelling is usually *-tion*:

addition	edition	ration
ambition	emotion	solution
audition	location	station
caution	notion	taxation
donation	petition	vacation
duration	position	vocation

But nouns based on words ending in *-ss* are spelt *-ssion*:

aggression	digression	profession
compression	expression	repression
concussion	impression	succession
depression	obsession	suppression
discussion	oppression	transgression

When the ending comes after an *l* the spelling is *-sion*:

compulsion	expulsion	repulsion
convulsion	propulsion	revulsion
emulsion		

When the ending comes after an *n* the spelling is often *-sion*:

apprehension	declension	extension
ascension	dimension	pretension
comprehension	dissension	suspension
condescension	expansion	tension

But some words are spelt *-ntion*:

abstention	contravention	mention
attention	detention	prevention
contention	intention	retention

When the ending comes after an *r* the spelling is often *-sion*:

aspersion	diversion	incursion
aversion	excursion	submersion
conversion	immersion	subversion
dispersion	perversion	version

After other consonants (usually *c*, *p*, or *s*) the ending is usually *-tion*:

absorption	digestion	obstruction
affection	disruption	perception
attraction	distinction	presumption
collection	exception	reception
congestion	exemption	redemption
connection	exhaustion	satisfaction
deception	indigestion	subscription
description	interruption	suggestion

There are two common words that end in *-cion*: *coercion, suspicion*.

**Dropping or keeping a
silent -*e* when adding
a suffix**

5 Dropping or keeping a silent -*e* when adding a suffix

If the suffix begins with a consonant you normally just add the suffix:

amuse	amusement
hope	hopeless
house	houseful
prince	princedom
supple	suppleness

If the suffix begins with a vowel, you usually drop a silent *e* at the end of a word:

arrange	arranger
blue	bluish
guide	guidance
reverse	reversal

But see also the lists of words ending in -*able* on page 78.

6 Double and single letters

abbreviation
accelerate
accessible
accessory
accidentally
accommodation
accomplish
additional
address
aggravate
aggression
aggressive
announcement
annulment
anoint
appearance
appropriate
beginner
beginning
billionaire
college
colossal
commemorate
committee
corroborate
curriculum
desiccated
deterrent
disappear
 (= *dis-* + *appear*)
disappoint
 (= *dis-* + *appoint*)
disapprove
 (= *dis-* + *approve*)
dissatisfied
 (= *dis-* + *satisfied*)
dissect
dissipated
drunkenness
 (= *drunken* + *-ness*)

eligible
embarrass
exaggerate
fulfil (*fulfill* in AmE)
grammar
happening
harass
illegible
imminent
immortal
 (= *im-* + *mortal*)
install
 (but *instalment*)
instil (*instill* is
 also correct)
irrelevant
marriage
marvel
meanness
 (= *mean* + *-ness*)
millennium
millionaire
misspell
 (= *mis-* + *spell*)
necessary
occasion
occasionally
occurrence
omission
omit
opponent
parallel
patrol
pedal
possess
possession
preference
questionnaire
recommend
reference

referral
remit
resurrect
saccharine
scurrilous
sheriff
skilful
 (*skillful* in AmE)
subterranean
success
successful
succession
successive
suddenness
 (= *sudden* + *-ness*)
supercilious
symmetrical
tariff
terrible
titillate
tobacco
tranquillity
 (*tranquility* in
 AmE)
transmit
threshold
 (but *withhold*)
trespasser
tyranny
unnecessary
 (= *un-* + *necessary*)
vaccination
vicissitude
wagon (*waggon* is
 also correct)
wholly
withhold
 (but *threshold*)
woollen (*woolen* in
 AmE)

7 Adding endings to words

7.1 adding -s or -es

You do this to make plural nouns (*cats*, *boxes*) and to make verb inflections (*stops*, *catches*).

Normally you add *s*, but when the word ends in -*s*, -*x*, -*z*, -*sh*, or -*ch* (pronounced as in *church*), you add -*es*:

count	counts
adore	adores
bus	buses
fix	fixes
buzz	buzzes
slash	slashes
church	churches
munch	munches

There are special rules for words that end in -*o* and -*y*:

-o

If it is a verb (a doing word) you add -*es*:

go	goes
veto	vetoes
video	videoes

If it is a noun (a naming word) it is less straightforward, because you sometimes add -s and sometimes -es. Some dictionaries allow either spelling for many words, especially for newer words of foreign origin. The plurals given here are the forms that are generally preferred.

Plurals in -os

Singular	Plural
avocado	avocados
banjo	banjos
casino	casinos
cello	cellos
concerto	concertos or concerti
contralto	contraltos
dodo	dodos
dynamo	dynamos
ego	egos
embryo	embryos
fiasco	fiascos
flamingo	flamingos
fresco	frescos
gigolo	gigolos
hairdo	hairdos
hippo	hippos
kilo	kilos
kimono	kimonos
libretto	librettos or libretti

Singular	Plural
manifesto	manifestos
memo	memos
peccadillo	peccadillos
photo	photos
piano	pianos
piccolo	piccolos
proviso	provisos
radio	radios
rhino	rhinos
silo	silos
solo	solos
soprano	sopranos
stiletto	stilettos
studio	studios
tiro	tiros
tobacco	tobaccos
video	videos
virago	viragos
yo-yo	yo-yos
zero	zeros

Plurals in *-oes*

Singular	Plural
buffalo	buffaloes
cargo	cargoes
domino	dominoes
echo	echoes
embargo	embargoes
ghetto	ghettoes
go	goes
grotto	grottoes
halo	haloes
hero	heroes
innuendo	innuendoes
mango	mangoes
memento	mementoes
mosquito	mosquitoes
motto	mottoes
Negro	Negroes
no	noes
portico	porticoes
potato	potatoes
salvo (= firing of guns)	salvoes
tomato	tomatoes
tornado	tornadoes
torpedo	torpedoes
veto	vetoes
volcano	volcanoes

-y

The rules for nouns and verbs are the same.

If the *y* comes after a consonant, you change the *y* to *-ies* (and also *-ied* for the past tense of verbs):

ally	allies
baby	babies
dynasty	dynasties
envy	envies
fly	flies
library	libraries
spy	spies
story	stories
trophy	trophies

If the y comes after a vowel (usually a or e or o), you add -s:

lay	lays
dismay	dismays
journey	journeys
buy	buys
toy	toys

Adding -s to nouns ending in -f and -fe

You normally change -f or -fe to -ves:

calf	calves
knife	knives
shelf	shelves

But if the final -*f* comes after two vowels, especially -*ief* and -*oof*, the plural form ends in -*fs*:

belief	beliefs
chief	chiefs
handkerchief	handkerchiefs
oaf	oafs
proof	proofs
roof	roofs

Adding -s to nouns ending in -i

You normally just add the -s:

alibi	alibis
coati	coatis
mini	minis
ski	skis
taxi	taxis

For other plural forms of words of foreign origin, e.g. *appendix* and *cactus*, see page 113.

Adding -s to nouns ending in -ful

Nouns like *cupful* and *handful* have plural forms ending in -*fuls*, e.g. *cupfuls*, *handfuls*. See page 110.

7.2 adding -ed and -ing to verbs

You add -*ed* to make a verb refer to the past (*she looked beautiful / have you looked?*), and you add -*ing* to make the form you need in a sentence such as *why are you laughing?*

If the verb ends in -*e* you usually drop this: *adore, adored, adoring; stare, stared, staring*

If the verb ends in a consonant (chiefly *b, d, f, g, l, m, n, p, r, s, t, z*) preceded by a single-letter vowel (e.g. *rap* but not *reap*, *refer* but not *appear*) you often have to double the consonant:

■ when the verb has only one syllable:

dab	dabbed	dabbing
stop	stopped	stopping

But if the consonant is preceded by more than one vowel you do not double the consonant:

daub	daubed	daubing
stoop	stooped	stooping

■ when the verb has more than one syllable and the stress on the final syllable:

allot	allotted	allotting
refer	referred	referring

But when the stress is on an earlier part of the word you do not double the final consonant:

benefit	benefited	benefiting
budget	budgeted	budgeting
deafen	deafened	deafening
gallop	galloped	galloping
pardon	pardoned	pardoning
target	targeted	targeting

Note also: *bigoted; cricketing, cricketer; faceted (as in multi-faceted); gardening; helmeted; rickety; wainscoted, wainscoting.*

But two words ending in -*p* double the *p* despite the early stress:

kidnap   kidnapped   kidnapping

worship   worshipped   worshipping

If the verb ends in *l*, you always double the *l*:

pedal   pedalled   pedalling

travel   travelled   travelling

(But note that in American English, the l is not doubled, i.e. *pedaled* and *traveled*.)

If the verb ends in *s*, a single *s* is more usual, although doubled forms are also found and are not wrong:

bias   biased *or* biassed   biasing *or* biassing

focus   focused *or* focussed   focusing *or* focussing

If the verb ends in *c* preceded by a single-letter vowel, you change *c* to *ck* (there are not many of these):

frolic   frolicked

magic   magicked

panic   panicked

If the verb ends in *y* coming after a consonant, you change the *y* to -*ied* :

cry   cried

espy   espied

But if the *y* comes after a vowel (usually *a* or *e* or *o*), you just add -*ed*:

dismay   dismayed

journey   journeyed

employ   employed

Note the following verbs which are 'irregular', i.e. behave in a special way:

lay   laid

pay   paid

say   said

If the verb ends in -ie (e.g. *die*, *untie*) you change *ie* to *y* when you add -*ing*:

belie   belying

die   dying

lie   lying

untie   untying

Note that the verb *dye* has a form *dyeing*, to distinguish it from *dying* from *die*.

7.3 A choice between -*t* and -*ed*

Some verbs of one syllable ending in *l*, *m*, *n*, or *p* can form past tenses and past participles ending in -*ed* or -*t*:

burn   burned *or* burnt

dream   dreamed *or* dreamt

dwell   dwelled *or* dwelt

lean   leaned *or* leant

leap   leaped *or* leapt

learn   learned *or* learnt

smell   smelled *or* smelt

spell   spelled *or* spelt

spill   spilled *or* spilt

spoil   spoiled *or* spoilt

Both forms are correct, but the -*t* spelling tends to be more common for past participles used as adjectives, e.g. *burnt food* as distinct from *we burned the food*.

Some verbs have -*t* forms only:

build	built
creep	crept
deal	dealt
feel	felt
keep	kept
kneel	knelt (also *kneeled* in AmE)
leave	left
lend	lent
send	sent
spend	spent

7.4 adding -*er* and -*est* to adjectives and adverbs

Adjectives and adverbs also have endings to give them special meanings. These endings are -*er* and -*est*: *smaller* means 'more small' and *smallest* means 'most small'.

You can add these endings to most adjectives and adverbs of one syllable, words of two syllables ending in *y* (such as *happy*) and their negative forms (*unhappy*), and a few other two-syllable words such as *common* and *pleasant*.

These endings are usually added without any further change, but there are a few special types:

- If the word ends in a single consonant (chiefly *b, d, f, g, l, m, n, p, r, s, t, z*) preceded by a single-letter vowel, the consonant is doubled: *hot, hotter, hottest*.

- If the word ends in *y* preceded by a consonant, the *y* is changed to *i*: *dry, drier, driest; happy, happier, happiest*.

■ If the word ends in a silent (unpronounced) *e*, the *e* is dropped: *late, later, latest; supple, suppler, supplest.*

■ If the word has two syllables and the second syllable ends in a single consonant, this is not normally doubled: *common, commoner, commonest.* An exception is *cruel*, which normally doubles the *l*: *crueller, cruellest.* There are not many words in this category.

8 Adding suffixes

8.1 Adding -ly

To make an adverb from an adjective you can normally just add -ly: *large, largely; quick, quickly*.

■ If the adjective ends in -y preceded by a consonant, the y normally changes to i: *happy, happily; noisy, noisily*.

■ The same applies to adjectives ending in -ey preceded by a consonant: *cagey, cagily; pricey, pricily*.

■ But short adjectives of only one syllable behave unpredictably, and there is no rule: *coy, coyly; dry, drily; gay, gaily; shy, shyly, wry, wryly*.
Note also: *daily* (which is also an adjective).

■ If the adjective ends in a consonant followed by -le, -le changes to -ly: *horrible, horribly; noble, nobly*.

■ If the adjective ends in -ic you add -ally: *drastic, drastically; heroic, heroically; tragic, tragically*.
There is one common exception: *public, publicly*.

There are quite a large number of adjectives that already end in -ly, e.g. *costly, ghostly, manly, orderly, silly*. In theory these form adjectives in -lily, but since words like *costlily* and (worse) *orderlily* are difficult to say they are normally avoided. You can always say (for example) *in an orderly way* instead.

8.2 Adding -ness

There are not so many problems with -ness. The main area of difficulty is with words ending in -y preceded by a consonant. Here, the rule with -ness is the same as the one for -ly: *happy, happily, happiness*.

One-syllable words like *coy* and *dry* just add -ness: *coyness, dryness, wryness*.

An exception is *busyness* (= the state of being busy), which keeps its final *-y* to distinguish it from the more familiar noun *business*.

Note that the same general rule applies to nouns ending in *-ment*: *accompany, accompaniment; merry, merriment*.

Words ending in *-n* have a double *n* when you add *-ness*: *meanness, suddenness*. It is common to find words like this spelt wrongly.

8.3 Adding *-er*

This suffix makes words meaning 'someone or something that does something' (e.g. *builder, opener*). Most of these words are straightforward, but there are occasional problems with single consonants (chiefly *b, d, f, g, l, m, n, p, r, s, t, z*) at the ends of words.

The pattern is the same as for the verb endings *-ed* and *-ing*:

- If the word has one syllable like *cut* and *tap* you double the consonant: *cutter, tapper*.

- If the word has more than one syllable you double the consonant when the stress is on the final syllable: *beginner, bedsitter*, but *cricketer, listener, prisoner*.
  Two important exceptions to this pattern are *kidnapper* and *worshipper*, which have a stress on the first syllable but still double the *p*.

- If the final consonant is *l* it is always doubled in British English: *reveller, traveller*. (But American English, more consistently, prefers *reveler* and *traveler*.)

- Words ending in *-y* preceded by a consonant normally change the *y* to *i*: *copier, drier*.

- Words ending in *-y* (preceded by a vowel) , *w*, or *x* simply add the suffix: *destroyer*.

8.4 Adding *-ful*

The following list includes some of the most common words ending in *-ful*, but there are many others:

Adjectives

bashful	forceful	neglectful	sorrowful
beautiful	fruitful	painful	spiteful
boastful	gainful	peaceful	stressful
cheerful	graceful	pitiful	successful
colourful	grateful	playful	tactful
delightful	harmful	plentiful	tasteful
doubtful	hateful	powerful	tearful
dreadful	helpful	remorseful	thankful
eventful	hopeful	reproachful	thoughtful
faithful	merciful	rightful	trustful
fanciful	mindful	scornful	useful
fateful	mournful	shameful	wishful
fearful	needful	sinful	wonderful

Nouns

armful	bowlful	glassful	pocketful
bagful	boxful	handful	roomful
barrelful	bucketful	houseful	shopful
basketful	carful	jugful	spoonful
bellyful	cupful	mouthful	stomachful
bottleful	earful	plateful	tubeful

Nouns ending in *-ful* have plural forms ending in *-fuls*:

cupful	cupfuls
handful	handfuls
spoonful	spoonfuls

9 Two consonants pronounced as one

Some words begin with combinations of two consonants that are pronounced as one (as with *ch* in *chronic* and *kn* in *knife*).

If you cannot find a word under the expected phonetic spelling, try the alternative beginnings shown in the following table:

c = k	ch	chronic
f	ph	phone
g	gh	ghetto
n	gn, kn, pn	gnu, knave, pneumatic
s	ps	psychology
r	wr	wrestle

The following are the most common words that begin with *gh*, *gn*, *kn*, *mn*, *pn*, *ps*, and *wr*:

ghetto	knead	knuckle	wrest
ghost	knee	pneumatic	wrestle
ghostly	kneel	pneumonia	wretched
ghoul	knickers	psychiatric	wriggle
gnarled	knife	(and other	wring
gnash	knight	psych- words)	wrinkle
gnat	knit	wrack	wrist
gnaw	knob	wrangle	writ
gnome	knock	wrap	write
gnostic	knoll	wreathe	writhe
gnu	knot	wreck	wrong
knack	know	wren	wrought
knave	knowledge	wrench	wry

dh- occurs in a few words of mainly Indian or Arabic origin: *dharma* (religious concept), *dhobi* (person who does washing), *dhoti* (loincloth), *dhow* (ship).

mn- occurs in *mnemonic* (something that aids memory).

ts- occurs in words from Japanese, especially *tsunami* (a high sea wave), and in words of African origin, e.g. *tsetse* (fly).

10 Other words with silent consonants

autumn	island
bomb	isle
comb	mortgage
corps (from French)	plumb
debt	plumber
doubt	receipt
indict	solemn
indictment	sword

l in some words, e.g.

balm	palm
calf	qualm
calm	should
could	talk
folk	walk
half	would

t in some words, e.g.

castle	often (*in this case, the t is*
fasten	*sometimes pronounced*)
listen	soften

and many words with *-gh-*, e.g.

eight	might
fight	night
flight	plight
freight	right
height	tight
light	weight

11 Words of foreign origin

These often have letter sequences that are not typical of English generally, such as ending in an unusual vowel or having *k* where we would expect *ck*

aficionado	flak	kosher	tandoori
balalaika	jodhpurs	kowtow	tortilla
basenji	kamikase	ombudsman	totem
batik	kebab	pagoda	trek
bungalow	khaki	schmaltz	yacht
catamaran	kiosk	sombrero	yak
fjord	koala	spaghetti	yeti

Some words, despite their familiarity in English, retain the accents they have in the source language, especially when these help to clarify a non-English pronunciation, e.g. *café*, *blasé*.

But accents are disappearing when they are not needed to help with the pronunciation, e.g. *role*, *gateau*.

Some words of foreign origin have special plural forms, or more than one possible form:

Nouns having Latin and Greek endings

addendum	addenda
apex	apices *or* apexes
appendix	appendixes *or* appendices
aquarium	aquaria *or* aquariums
arena	arenas
automaton	automata
basis	bases
cactus	cacti
compendium	compendia *or* compendiums
consortium	consortia *or* consortiums

crematorium	crematoria *or* crematoriums
crisis	crises
crux	cruxes *or* cruces
encomium	encomia
focus	focuses *or* foci
formula	formulas *or (technical)* formulae
genus	genera
gymnasium	gymnasiums *or* gymnasia
helix	helices
index	indexes *or* (technical) indices
matrix	matrices *or* matrixes
maximum	maxima *or* maximums
momentum	momenta *or* momentums
moratorium	moratorium *or* moratoria
nucleus	nuclei
oasis	oases
referendum	referendums *or* referenda
stigma	stigmas *or (technical)* stigmata
stratum	strata
thesis	theses
vortex	vortices

Nouns of French origin ending in -*eau*

chateau	chateaux
gateau	gateaux
plateau	plateaux (*also* plateaus)
tableau	tableaux

12 Hyphens

Hyphens have a double function in general use as a part of spelling and a part of punctuation. They can either be a permanent part of the spelling of a compound word, or they can link words when these occur in special positions in a sentence.

12.1 Hyphens in compound words

Compound words are words like *tabletop*, *road hog*, and *best-seller*, which are made from two other words, typically two nouns (naming words) or a noun and adjective (describing word).

There are no hard and fast rules about when and when not to use a hyphen in words like these, and you will often see the same compound word spelt in each of the three ways in different places. The important point is to remain consistent in your own writing, so that the same compound doesn't appear in different forms in the same document.

Compounds with hyphens are much less common than they used to be. Even when putting two words together causes a long sequence of consonants, these are more often written and printed as one word, for example *jackknife* (four consonants) and *breaststroke* (five consonants).

You should avoid compounds that would be absurdly long as one word by spelling them as two words, e.g. *colour supplement*, *filling station*.

It is more usual to spell a compound as two words when these keep their separate identity and meaning more strongly in the resulting compound, e.g. *fire door*, *ground speed*, *killer instinct*, *panic attack*.

A hyphen is still used when there is a grammatical relationship between the two words that form the compound, as in *load-bearing* (= bearing a load) , *punch-drunk* (= 'drunk' from punches), and *go-ahead* (= permission to go ahead). In these compounds, the words can be unwrapped into a phrase or sentence, as distinct from routine compounds which simply mean 'an x that is y' (e.g. *start date*) or 'an x that has to do with y' (e.g. *street lamp*).

12.2 Hyphens with prefixes

Prefixes are groups of letters, such as *re-* and *un-*, that you can add to words to change their meaning or make new words (as in *recall* and *unscientific*). You can read about them on page 43.

You need a hyphen:

- if the word coming after the prefix begins with a capital letter (e.g. *non-Christian, un-American*);

- when a prefix ends in a vowel (e.g. *re-, micro-*) and is joined to a word beginning with the same vowel or one that might confuse the sound (e.g. *re-examine, micro-organism*);

- to distinguish an ordinary meaning from a special one, e.g. *re-cover* = 'to give a new cover to' and *re-sign* = 'to sign again' (*recover* and *resign* have special meanings).

The two prefixes *ex-* and *non-* tend to be followed by a hyphen routinely, e.g. *ex-directory, ex-president, non-delivery, non-event, non-smoking*. This is because these words can look long and clumsy if they are spelt as single words.

12.3 Hyphens as links

One very important and useful role the hyphen has is to make the meaning clear when you get a row of nouns, or nouns and other words, and you need to show which go with which.

Here are some more examples of useful hyphens that show the links between words and avoiding confusion of meaning:

a big-game hunter
twenty-odd people
extra-marital sex

a small-business adviser
a well-known actor
an up-to-date record (*but* the record is up to date)
a lower-than-average turnout (*but* the turnout was lower than average)
a cast-iron excuse

| # 13 Apostrophes

Apostrophes are mostly a matter of punctuation, but they can also affect permanent aspects of spelling:

- In contracted words such as *can't, don't, I'll, wouldn't, they've,* etc., the apostrophes represent missing letters.

- In words such as *fo'c'sle, ne'er-do-well,* and *rock 'n' roll,* the apostrophes again represent missing letters.

- In words like *cello* (short for *violoncello*) and *flu* (short for *influenza*) it is no longer usual to put an apostrophe to represent missing letters at the beginnings and ends of words.

- In plurals like *MPs,* the *2000s,* etc., the apostrophe is now usually omitted.

- Ordinary plurals like *videos* and *apples* should not have an apostrophe (the so-called 'grocer's apostrophe', e.g. *apple's 30p a pound*), although the plurals of some short words ending in a vowel can have an apostrophe for clarity, e.g. *do's* (as in *do's and don'ts*).

For the possessive apostrophe, as in *a day's journey* and *their parents' room*, see Chapter 4, Endings and changes, on page 37.

14 Spelling names and proper nouns

Names of people and places are called proper nouns because they are 'proper' (in the old meaning of 'belonging specially') to one particular person or thing. They are normally spelt with a capital initial letter.

Although some proper names are special uses of ordinary words (e.g. *Smith, Baker, the New Forest*), very many are special words, either made from ordinary words (e.g. *Oxford, Castleford*) or having no obvious connection with ordinary words (e.g. *London, Moscow*).

Some personal names are spelt in different ways (e.g. *Ann, Anne; Catherine, Katharine, Katherine; Jonathan, Jonathon, Jonothan*). The same applies to some surnames (e.g. *Allan, Allen; Macdonald, McDonald; Ramsay, Ramsey*). Make sure you know the right form for the person you are addressing or referring to.

Remember that foreign names often contain unusual letter sequences, e.g. *sch* in German (as in *Messerschmitt*). Sometimes you can remember a spelling more easily if you find out what the name means in the source language (and you don't have to speak the language to do this!), e.g. *Casanova* is based on Italian *casa nova* which means 'new house'.

Some country names change their spelling for political or historical reasons, e.g. *Belorussia* to *Belarus*.

Here is a list of some names that are often misspelt:

Afghanistan
Antarctic
Auschwitz
Bartholomew
Beaulieu (*pronounced* **byoo**-li)
Buddha
Cincinnati
Colombia (*in S. America*)
Columbia (*in Canada, and* District of Columbia *in Washington DC*)
Copenhagen
Dostoevsky

Frances (*female personal name*)
Francis (*male personal name, also used as a surname*)
Gandhi
Grieg
Guatemala
Guinevere (*wife of King Arthur*)
Gwynedd (*in Wales*)
Heidelberg
Huguenot
Johannesburg
Luxembourg
Massachusetts
Mediterranean
Michelangelo
Mississippi
Muhammad
Neanderthal
Nuremberg
Nureyev
Peloponnese (*in Greece*)
Pennsylvania
Philip (*but the surname is usually* Phillips)
Piccadilly
Pyrenees
Romania
Roosevelt
St Petersburg
Scheherazade
Shakespeare
Solzhenitsyn
Strasbourg
Sidney (*personal name*)
Sydney (*in Australia*)
Worcester

15 Capitalization in other words

Some words have capital initial letters even though they are not proper names. The most important uses of capitals are:

- in personal names, e.g. *Lisa*, *Rajiv*;

- in titles of books, plays, pieces of music, pictures, newspapers, etc.;

- in titles of people, e.g. *the Bishop of Durham*, *Her Majesty the Queen*;

- in words for particular institutions, e.g. *the Government*, *the State*, *the Crown*, *the Church*, *the Labour Party*, *Islam*, etc.;

- in geographical descriptions that are recognized names, e.g. *Northern Ireland* (but *northern England*, which is purely geographical);

- in names of special days and festivals, e.g. *Easter*, *Boxing Day*, *Diwali*.

16 British and American differences

The British and American forms of English have gone their own way for over three hundred years, and so it is not surprising that they have evolved some major differences of spelling. Some of these are simply 'one-off', as with British *manoeuvre* / American *maneuver* and British *pyjamas* / American *pajamas*.

Other differences are more systematic, and apply to whole classes of words; for example, many words ending in *-our* in British English end in *-or* in American English. Some of the American differences in fact preserve older forms that were once used in Britain too but have changed since; for example, the spelling *theater*.

In some spellings American practice tries to remove the anomalies and inconsistencies that are present in British spelling. For example, the letter *l* at the end of words behaves more like other consonants in spellings such as *counseling* (British *counselling*), *traveler* (British *traveller*), and *fulfill* (British *fulfil*).

The most important differences between British and American spellings are:

■ The vowels *-ae-* and *-oe-* are usually reduced to *-e-* in American spelling (as in *archeology* and *ameba*). This is beginning to have an effect on British spelling too: for example, *encyclopedia* (with *-e-* instead of *-ae-*) is now very common.

■ *-ense* is used instead of British *-ence* as a noun ending (as in *defense*, *license*, and *pretense*).

■ Noun and verb differences of the kind listed on page 77 are not so rigorously applied in American English. For example, the spelling *practice* is used for the verb (compare British *practise*) as well as the noun.

■ *-er* is used instead of British *-re* as a noun ending in many words (as in *center* and *theater*). But some words, for example *acre*, *massacre*, *mediocre*, and *ogre*, are the same in both British and American English.

■ *-or* is used instead of *-our* as a noun ending (as in *color* and *harbor*).

■ the final *l* of verbs in which the stress is not on the final syllable, such as *rival* and *travel*, do not double in the forms ending
in *-ed*, *-ing*, and *-er* as they do in British spelling (so *rivaled* and
traveler instead of British *rivalled* and *traveller*). The *l* is however
doubled when the stress is placed on its syllable in speech,
e.g. *installment* (British *instalment*) and *skillful* (British *skilful*).

■ The British ending *-ogue* is written in American spelling as *-og*
(as in *analog* and *catalog*).

■ The British spelling *programme* is written as *program* in
American English, and this spelling is standard on both sides of
the Atlantic in the context of computing.

■ In British spelling some verbs can be spelt with either *-ize* or
-ise (e.g. *privatize* or *privatise*), but these are always written with
-ize in American spelling.

■ In American spelling *z* is used instead of *s* in some other words,
e.g. *analyze* and *cozy*.

Glossary

Technical terms have been avoided as far as possible, but there are a few that are needed to make the explanations clear. These are explained where they are used in the text, and they are listed here for general information.

adjective a word that describes another word, e.g. *blue, horrible, pleasant*

adverb a word that qualifies a verb or adjective, e.g. *quickly, very*. A word such as *only* can be an adjective (as in *the only one*) and an adverb (as in *I only asked*).

consonant any of the letters *b, c, d, f, g, h, j, k, l, m, n, p, q, r, s, t, v, w, x, z*. The letter *y* is a consonant when it is sounded as in *year* and *yoke*, but is a vowel in words such as *rhythm* and *tyre*.

digraph a pair of letters pronounced as one sound, e.g. *ch, ph*

diphthong a vowel sound that changes within the same syllable, e.g. *ai* in *main*, *ou* in *sound*, or *i* in *mine*

homophone each of two or more words that are pronounced the same way but spelt differently, e.g. *pair, pare,* and *pear*

inflection a change to the ending of a word to make it fit its grammatical context, e.g. *-ed* and *-ing* in verbs or *-s* and *-es* forming plurals of nouns

long vowel a vowel such as the *ea* in *mean* or the *i* in *fight*, as distinct from the short vowels in *men* and *fit*

mnemonic a way of remembering something, usually a rhyme or catchy set of words associated with the thing to be remembered

noun	a noun that names a person or thing, e.g. *house, George, happiness*
past participle	a form of a verb used with *be* or *have*, such as *killed, burnt*, or *spoken*, or as a kind of adjective, as in *the burnt cakes*
possessive	a word that indicates ownership or a similar relation, e.g. a noun as in *the **boys'** room* or ***London's** river*, or a word such as *my, her, hers, their, theirs*, etc.
prefix	a number of letters added to the beginning of a word to change its meaning, e.g. *re-* in *remarry* and *un-* in *unhappy*
preposition	a word such as *in, on*, or *over*, which stands before a noun as in *the book **on** the table*
pronoun	a word such as *I, he, me*, and *us* which is used instead of a noun. Possessive pronouns are words such as *mine* and *ours*
proper noun	a noun that refers to one particular person, place, or thing and is spelt with a capital initial, e.g. *Europe, Titanic, Shakespeare*
short vowel	a vowel with a short sound, such as the *e* in *men* or the *i* in *fit*, as distinct from the vowels with a longer sound as in *mean* and *feet*, and the diphthongs (see **diphthong** above) in *mine* and *fight*
stem	the part of a word that does not change and to which inflections, prefixes, and suffixes can be added, e.g. *burn* in *burner* and *burning* and *self* in *selfish* and *selflessness*
suffix	a number of letters added to the end of a word to change its meaning, e.g. *-ly* in *equally* and *-er* in *opener*
syllable	a part of a word that can be pronounced separately, e.g. *but* and *ter* in *butter*
verb	a word that describes an action or state, e.g. *become, move, remain, take*
vowel	any of the letters *a, e, i, o, u*, and sometimes *y* (as in *rhythm*: see **consonant** above)

Further reading

Titles marked * are available as paperbacks

Dictionaries

The Concise Oxford Dictionary (revised tenth edition, Oxford, 2001)

The Oxford Compact English Dictionary (second edition, Oxford, 2000): a shortened version of the *Concise*, which some readers may find easier to use for basic spelling

(Similar dictionaries are published by Chambers Harrap, HarperCollins, Penguin Books, and others. Choose one that suits you best, and bear in mind that you may need more than one for different purposes.)

*The Oxford Spelling Dictionary (second edition, Oxford, 1995): a listing of words and their inflections, with guidance on word-division in printing

The Oxford Dictionary for Writers and Editors (second edition, 2000): covers many difficult and confused spellings and includes proper names

Reference books on language

Tom McArthur, *The Concise Oxford Companion to the English Language* (Oxford, 1998): includes many articles on spelling and spelling features

*David Crystal, *The Cambridge Encyclopedia of the English Language*
(Cambridge, 1995): has much to say on writing and spelling,
with historical background and good illustrations

Some more advanced books on spelling and word formation in English

G. H. Vallins, *Spelling* (second edition, London, 1965)

D. G. Scragg, *A History of English Spelling* (Manchester, 1974)

D. Thompson, *Spelling and Punctuation* (Oxford, 1981)

*Laurie Bauer, *English Word-Formation* (Cambridge, 1983)

*John Mountford, *An Insight into English Spelling* (London, 1998)

Extracts

Extract on page 13 taken from *The Oxford Compact English Dictionary* (2nd edn, Oxford, 2000) page 24.

Extract from The Squire's Tale on page 49, from *The Riverside Chaucer* (3rd edn, Oxford, 1988).

Extract on page 51 from the *Oxford English Dictionary* (2nd edn, Oxford, 1989).

Index

Bold page numbers are used for the reference section and glossary
Italics are used to show parts of words
For endings such as *-ly*, *-ness*, and *-ful*, see also pages 56–7

accents **113**
adjectives 12, **124**
  forming adverbs from adjectives **108**
  in compound words **115–16**
  -er and *-est* forms 42, **106–7**
  forming nouns from adjectives 37, 44, **108–9**
adverbs **124**
  formed from adjectives **108**
  endings 42, **106–7**
alternative spellings 9, 10, 16, 37–40, **78–95**
American spellings 7, **104**, **122–3**
Anglo-Saxon words 32, 49–50
apostrophes **118**
  standing for missing letters 29–30, **118**
  forming possessive words 29, 41, **118, 125**

beginnings of words 13, 21–2
  see also prefixes
British and American spellings 7, **122–3**

capitalization **119, 121**
compound words **115–16**
confusable words 17, 28–33, **62–76, 124**
consonants **124**
  clusters and pairs 23, 48
  doubling of consonants 11, 17, 36, 46
  silent consonants 48, 51, **111–12**
  single consonants 7, 11, 27, 46, **97, 104**
  two consonants pronounced as one **111–12**

dictionaries 10, 11–13, 40
digraphs 52, **124**
diphthongs 23, **124**
double and single letters 27, **97**
doubling of consonants, *see* consonants

endings 11, 22, 36–46, **98–107**
  see also inflections; plurals of nouns; suffixes

foreign words 32–3, **113–14**

glossary of terms **124–5**
grammar affecting spelling 41–3, 53
Greek 33, 50, **113–14**

history of spelling 47–54
homophones 28–31, 53, **124**
hyphens 44, **115–17**

inflections 41–3
  see also endings

Latin 32, 35–6, 40, 47, 50
  plurals of Latin nouns 33, **113–14**
Latin and Greek words 50
letter clusters 23
letters and sounds 47–8
look-spell-cover-write-check method 17

mnemonics 18–19, **111, 124**

nouns 12, **125**
  formed from adjectives and verbs 37–40, 44–6, **91–2, 108–9**
  in compound words **115–16**
  noun endings 41–3, **98–107**
  spelling of nouns and related verbs **77**
  proper nouns **119–20, 125**
  see also plurals of nouns

origins of words 30, 32–3

phonetic alphabet 52–4
places, names of **119–21**
plurals of nouns 33, 41–2, **98–102, 110**
  of foreign origin **102, 113–14**
possessive forms 29, 41, **118, 125**
prefixes 27, 35, 43–4, **116, 125**
  non- 44, **116**
  re- 44, **116**
  un- 44, **116**
  see also beginnings
prepositions **125**
printing, effect on spelling 51
problem words **58–61**
pronunciation 49
proper nouns **119–20, 125**

reform of spelling 52–4
rules and patterns 9, 20, 41

silent letters 48, 51, **111–12**
  silent *-e* 26, 47, **96, 107**
single consonants, *see* consonants
sounds and letters 21–6, 47–8
spell-checkers 16–17
spelling reform 52–4
suffixes 43–5, **108–10, 125**
  -ly and *-ness* 44
  suffixes of foreign origin 33
  see also endings
syllables 34–5, **125**

technical words 33

verbs 12, **125**
  endings 41–3, 98, **101–6**
  spelling of verbs and related nouns **77**

vowels **125**
  clusters and pairs 23–6, 48
  long vowels 26, 49, **124**
  pairs of vowels with one sound 25
  short vowels 26, **125**